PEOPLE
MANAGEMENT
FOR SMALL BUSINESS

The Small Business Series

DAVID M. BROWNSTONE, *GENERAL EDITOR*

Credit and Collections
John W. Seder

Efficient Accounting and Record-Keeping
Dennis M. Doyle

Financing Your Business
Egon W. Loffel

How to Advertise and Promote Your Small Business
Gonnie McClung Siegel

How to Run a Successful Florist and Plant Store
Bram Cavin

How to Run a Successful Specialty Food Store
Douglass L. Brownstone

How to Run a Successful Restaurant
William L. Siegel

People Management for Small Business
William L. Siegel

Protecting Your Business
Egon W. Loffel

Successful Selling Skills for Small Business
David M. Brownstone

Tax-Planning Opportunities
Gerald F. Richards

PEOPLE MANAGEMENT FOR SMALL BUSINESS

William L. Siegel

A HUDSON GROUP BOOK

David M. Brownstone, *General Editor*

John Wiley & Sons, Inc.
New York   Chichester   Brisbane   Toronto

Copyright © 1978, by John Wiley & Sons, Inc.

All Rights reserved. Published simultaneously in Canada.

Reproduction or translation of any part of
this work beyond that permitted by Sections
107 and 108 of the 1976 United States Copyright
Act without the permission of the copyright
owner is unlawful. Requests for permission
or further information should be addressed to
the Permissions Department, John Wiley & Sons.

Library of Congress Cataloging in Publication Data

Siegel, William Laird.
  People management for small business.

  (Wiley small business series)
  "A Hudson Group book."
  1. Small business—Personnel management.
2. Personnel management. I. Title.
HF5549.S5858   658.3'03   77-27038
ISBN 0-471-04030-4

Produced and Designed by Ken Burke & Associates

10 9 8 7 6 5 4 3 2 1

Manufactured in the United States of America

CONTENTS

PEOPLE MANAGEMENT FOR SMALL BUSINESS

Introduction

EVERY TIME YOU WALK INTO A BUSINESS, YOU SEE PEOPLE—people making things, selling things, performing services. All businesses are based on people—even giant computer industries.

If you are just preparing to launch a small enterprise, you probably have only vague ideas about how to manage employees. This book is for you.

If you've operated a small business for years, you probably still have many questions about managing your employees. This book is for you also.

This book has one major theme—people management is something that takes plenty of caution and care. A small business owner pours a big chunk of earnings into paying for employees. So solid, productive workers are a must. A good employee will help a small business prosper and grow. A rotten employee can help destroy a small business.

This book is a practical guide to finding the best employees. It is divided into three parts:

- Hiring.
- Orientation and training.
- People management.

These are all extremely important functions which all small business owners with employees must be familiar with.

Discovering and hiring the employee is the first step. Selecting the correct person is vital. You need someone who can do the necessary work, and who can be trusted. Too many businesses are fatally hurt by incompetent or dishonest employees. The selection process is designed to hire the best and weed out the undesirables.

Training comes next. The new employee must be given the proper skills to do the job he or she was hired for. Training can't be approached as a hit-or-miss proposition.

Management is something that should start the minute the employee is formally hired. Good people management is tough and time-consuming, but worth every second. Proper management helps keep your employees working, and working productively.

All these steps are related. One without the other is a waste of time. You, the small business owner, must be aware of each element of people management. That is the purpose of this book.

Part I

HIRING

ONE

Getting the Right People for Your Business

Do You Really Need a New Employee?—Job Analysis /
The Job Description / What the Job Description Does

DURING HARVEY'S FIRST YEAR IN HIS OWN BUSINESS, HE got a kick out of reading the help-wanted columns in his Sunday paper, since he thought that placing an ad to attract a worker was a dimwitted waste of good money. After all, hadn't he gotten along nicely by sticking a cardboard sign in his display window saying "HELP WANTED"?

But after that first year, Harvey sat down with the black-and-white figures. The hard facts about his employee turnover stared him right in the eye. The longest an employee had stayed with him was four and a half months. During the past year he had hired and fired seven different people in one job.

Harvey began thinking about all the hassles, all the time, and all the money this kind of turnover was costing him. His entire business was disrupted. He no sooner had adjusted himself to an employee when the employee walked off the job. And then there were the two employees he caught stealing merchandise during the few weeks they had "worked" for him. Those weeks were deep in the red. In the end Harvey revised his hiring procedure—it was either that or close up.

Harvey's situation, unfortunately, is not unique among small businesses. How many times have you seen a tattered "Help Wanted" sign stuck in a window? And how many times have you seen it disappear and reappear?

But small business owners cry, "I'm not General Motors or AT&T. I don't have a huge personnel department. I can't afford to take time away from the business to look for employees. Besides, I only need a salesclerk—or someone to handle the cash register or stack boxes. Any fool can do that."

Sure. But any fool could rip you off, too. Employee theft is as serious as shoplifting in a small business. No small business can afford to be plundered.

It's amazing how many small businesses use slipshod hiring methods similar to Harvey's sign in the window. Industrial espionage, employee theft, strikes, management/labor disputes, faulty workmanship, alcoholism—small business owners think these are big and middle-sized companies' problems, when they start out. Then after a while many owners become hardened to theft, tardiness, poor workmanship, absenteeism, and turnover. "That's just the way things are these days—you can't get responsible help any more." Many owners are singing that old song and not paying any attention to the solutions to their very real problems.

Getting a good employee—the right employee—is not accomplished by hanging out a sign, followed by a shallow conversation with the potential employee. Everyone remembers old movies of the thirties and forties when The Hero tucks the old "Help Wanted" sign under his arm and saves a failing business owned by a gruff, kindly, but inept owner. It doesn't work that way very often nowadays—and it didn't then.

Of course, you can't expect an Einstein to become your clerk, dishwasher, stock boy, or cash register operator—but you can expect reasonably capable, honest employees. Dishonest or careless employees can hamstring any small business. Imagine a small marginal business losing hundreds of dollars a month into an employee's pocket. What's the logical result? One less small business.

It doesn't have to be that dramatic, either. A bad salesclerk can drive away enough customers to severely hurt a marginal business. How many times have you walked into a store, been snubbed by a salesperson, and never gone back? It happens all the time. Or an inefficient delivery person can tie up an entire operation by mixing up orders. And a resentful stock clerk can easily mangle an entire inventory. Sure, you can and probably will fire employees like these—after you discover what they have done. But where does that leave you? Either you or another employee will have to fill in until someone else can be hired. The result is a great deal of wasted effort, which spells lost profits. And if you put the old sign back in the window, chances are that you'll be the proud employer of another loser.

So hiring is important. And the flip side of the coin is that a really good employee is a gold mine to a small business. Many small business owners have employees who function as their right hands. If the owner gets sick or wants to take a vacation, no problem. He has a trustworthy employee who can do the job.

What it all boils down to is that good employees can help your business grow. Bad employees can send your business down the tube. The choice is yours.

DO YOU REALLY NEED A NEW EMPLOYEE?— JOB ANALYSIS

Jonathan realized one day that he seemed to spend a great deal of time calling employment agencies. His foreman asked for another person, so Jonathan called his favorite agency. His small machine shop now had twelve employees. Jonathan checked his records. Two years ago he had only had seven employees. And business had increased by just 15 percent. Why the huge jump in numbers?

The basic problem was that Jonathan had spent so much of his time worrying about the financial demands of his business that he had neglected the people working for him. He had delegated some management functions to one of his employees, and the result was a poor hiring policy. Jobs overlapped, and too many people spent too much of their day drinking coffee and waiting for work.

The flaw in Jonathan's business was that there was no real analysis of jobs. When the foreman felt things were getting busy, he just asked for another worker. The result was that Jonathan's business collected employees.

Before you go out and hire additional people, the first step is to know specifically what you're hiring them for. Sounds fundamental, doesn't it? But too many owners hire by instinct, not taking the time and effort to match the employee to the specific job. The result is a poor employee team, sloppy work, and high turnover.

So what's the first step? Simple. Understand your business' organization. Know every step of the different jobs that have to be performed. Understand how each job functions within the organization—how it affects other jobs. It boils down to taking a long, hard look at what makes your business tick. This is called *job analysis*.

Job analysis is important whether you're just starting out or have been in business for ten years. If you're still in the planning stages, you'll have to rely on estimates, which is a matter of taking the estimated figures and guessing how many people you'll need. For example, suppose you're planning to open a bookstore in a few months. How busy will you be? Take a look at your competition. Then look at your own estimates again. Determine how many duties you'll be able to perform on your own—then you'll know what your employees should do. If it's going to be a small bookstore specializing in paperbacks, you may need a single employee or even a couple of part-time workers. If your bookstore is to incorporate a hardcover section, a paperback section, a record department, a games department, and a sale area, you may need three or four full-time employees plus some part-time help. But again, know exactly what your employees will be doing before you hire them.

A job analysis for an established business is easier in some ways, but more difficult in others. It is easier because there are records to work from, revealing how much business has been done in the past and how much business will probably be done in the future. The owner of an established business also has some idea of what the employees have been doing. But it is often difficult to wade through misleading appearances in an established business. Everyone may look busy, but along the line one employee may be working hard at undoing what another worker has been doing. Or some workers may be engaged in a series of operations which should be eliminated.

How do you discover the true organization of your business? How do you perform a useful job analysis? Hopefully, you've

kept a tight rein on your business' activities. You know how slot
A gets filled and how slot B gets emptied. But you'll need to dig
a little deeper. Ask your employees about each job. Use a ques-
tionnaire to get their opinions. Also, ask them for suggestions.
Do they feel that hiring a new employee is a good idea? You
have to worry about fitting a new employee into the team. Because that's what small businesses are—a team. You shouldn't
upset your employees by springing a new employee on them—it
creates resentment and bitterness. In a small business, the
employees should be consulted. They know their jobs. They can
supply you with much useful information. And, in turn, they appreciate being made a part of the business process, something
more valuable than just a paid hand.

After gathering information, look over the hiring records.
What standards have you set in the past? Should those standards
continue? Are they too loose in some ways and too strict in
others? Let your experience be your guide and do what works
for you.

THE JOB DESCRIPTION

Job analysis is the information-gathering stage. The next step is
transforming the information into a written profile of the job,
called the *job description*. Actually, this profile has two parts:
job description and job specification. *Job description* delineates
the duties the employee is expected to perform on the job. *Job
specification* states employee qualifications—the educational
level, skills, experience, personal qualities, and physical qualities
he or she must have in order to qualify.

If you have trouble pinpointing the job, it may be a good idea
to go to your public library and examine the *Dictionary of Occupational Titles* published by the U.S. Employment Services,
which lists thousands of jobs.

For example, the description for "Salesman" in Volume I is:

Sells merchandise to business or industrial establishments, or to individuals, utilizing detailed knowledge of specific characteristics of merchandise, at sales office, store, showroom, or customer's home or place
of business. Calls on customer in person or by phone, or talks to
customer on sales floor. Displays merchandise, using samples or cat-

alog. Demonstrates article, emphasizing salable features. Estimates or quotes prices, credit terms, and trade-in allowances. Prepares forms and sales contracts. Prepares reports of business transactions and keeps expense accounts. May set up window displays and advertising posters. May collect payment of products sold. May install commercial, industrial, or household equipment and instruct buyer in use or operation.

This description of a salesman's duties runs the full gamut of selling activities. Reading the *Dictionary* gives you an overview of the government's definition of various occupations.

Volume II goes a step further than Volume I. It groups related jobs and classifies the abilities, vocational experience, and potential of workers. This volume may be helpful as a guide when you write your own job specifications.

The listing in Volume II of "Demonstration and Sales Work" is as follows:

Work Performed:
Worker activities in this group primarily involve using persuasive techniques to sell and/or demonstrate materials, products, or services, drawing upon some knowledge relevant to items or services sold. Some of these activities occur in retail, wholesale, or similar establishments, while some involve soliciting by telephone, going from door to door, or making appointments and visiting the customer to make sales. Demonstrations are made in many of the selling situations. Some demonstrating situations, however, do not involve making sales.

Worker Requirements:
An occupationally significant combination of: facility with words; ability to become familiar with the objects, material, or services involved; numerical facility and perception for clerical detail; drive and initiative; diplomacy and tact in dealing with people; and powers of persuasion.

Clues for Relating Applicants and Requirements:
Good grooming and attire.
Expressed preference for public-contact work.
Casual sales experience.
Poise and good vocabulary in an interview.

Training and Methods of Entry:
Employees will usually require the minimum of a high school education, with many requiring a college background or night school credits. At the college level, courses in business and administration, marketing, and related areas will give the individual excellent preparation. Many

larger organizations have training programs designed to develop the worker's ability as he learns.

Volume II also has a qualifications profile of workers' traits which can be useful when drawing up your job specifications.

Now, with all your information close at hand, and the example of the *Dictionary of Occupational Titles,* write your own job description, using only what is relevant for your business. Write the description in clear, concise language, trying to include every important aspect of the job. This job description is a map for you to follow, so make it understandable.

A sample job description for a salesclerk in a flower shop might look like this:

Position: Salesperson.
Supervisor: Store owner.
Duties:
- Handle all sales in the shop.
- Take phone orders.
- Arrange some displays.
- Assist with window displays.
- Write orders from customers, both phone and floor.
- Operate cash register.
- Help in stockroom on occasion, and do light cleaning and straightening.
- Work on any other assigned task.

Job specifications:
- Education: High school graduate preferred, but exceptions considered. Courses in floriculture helpful.
- *Experience:* Minimum of three months steady experience in retail sales.
- *Skills:* Must be able to work well with people; basic mathematical skills; pleasant phone voice.
- *Other:* Self-starter, personable, independent, cheerful, willing to pitch in and work on any assigned task.

You may want to add more information about the job or the type of personal characteristics you want for the job. Remember, this is your blueprint. Once you have the job description, you are ready to begin the search for an individual to fill it—a more complicated task.

WHAT THE JOB DESCRIPTION DOES

A written job description serves two purposes: It describes the job, and it tells the employee what his or her function will be in the company. Always remember that you are in charge, the one who is ultimately responsible for what your employees do—the buck stops with you. So for your own protection, know the operation of all jobs as well as or better than your employees. In most small businesses this is generally possible, since the owner has had to do every single function in order to make the business a success. Many a tycoon reminisces about sweeping up the floor in a once-struggling business. The problem now becomes communication. Too many owners, used to doing everything themselves, are unable to give their employees clear, concise instructions. A concrete job description, in black and white, eliminates many of these problems. Every job description should include a catch-all line requiring the employee to perform any assignment the owner asks. No small business can exist without this kind of job function overlap.

Job specification is also vital. You are arming yourself before the applicants start marching through your front door. What you need is the most qualified individual—in skills, experience, and attitudes. You'll rarely find your charted ideal—but with a clear picture of the perfect employee, you'll come much closer than if you were unprepared.

Too many small business owners make the mistake of generalizing when it's time to pick an employee. They wind up with underskilled or overqualified people—both unsatisfactory. The underskilled employee costs money by not producing quality work, and the overqualified employee is too expensive for the function. For example, a gas station owner makes a serious mistake in hiring a pumper to work as a general mechanic (see SBA illustration). And a fast-food restaurant specializing in precoated deep-fried chicken wastes money by hiring a highly skilled chef to stand over a deep fryer.

Of course, sometimes the best course is to hire a trainee and provide a solid training course—but that must be your decision, based on many personal factors. Regardless of your choice, both you and your new employee will be upset if job and worker

HIRING THE RIGHT MAN

1.KNOW WHAT YOU WANT NEW EMPLOYEE TO DO.

2.DECIDE WHAT SKILLS NEW EMPLOYEE WILL NEED TO DO THE JOBS YOU WANT HIM TO DO.

3.DON'T HIRE UNTIL YOU FIND AN EMPLOYEE WHO HAS THESE SKILLS.

DO THIS

don't match. The poor, harried gas pumper portrayed in the SBA cartoon will have nightmares about fixing hostile cars. And the skilled chef will dream of gourmet kitchens while he undercooks the chicken out of boredom.

Forearmed is forewarned when employee-hunting. Your job description is a good friend when you start talking to prospective employees. So do your homework beforehand. It will insure that both you and the applicants get a fair shake.

TWO

Finding the Perfect Employee

*Employment Agencies / Advertising / Schools / Labor
Unions and Organizations / Employee Referrals / Walk-ins /
Recruiting from Competitors / Organizations for the
Handicapped or Disadvantaged / Minorities /
Situation-Wanted Ads / Temporary Employment Agencies /
Family and Relatives*

WITH YOUR DREAM EMPLOYEE DANCING IN YOUR MIND, begin your search.

Actually, there are many ways of getting bodies into your business, especially during times of tight job markets and high unemployment. One company ran an unusual ad in the classified section of the *New York Times*. The ad described the response that another of the company's recent ads had produced. The response was staggering: More than 200 people, many with Ph.D.s, applied for a low-level economics job. This is typical of many others. And if you're located in an area of high unemployment, be prepared for an onslaught.

The point is that you should have no trouble getting people to apply for any job you want filled. But you need more than a warm body. You need a real candidate for the job—someone who is qualified and serious and motivated.

Unfortunately, in the meantime you also have to mind the store. You can't drop everything and become a full-time personnel manager. Be prepared to search for, screen, interview, and check the applicants by setting up your operation on home grounds. With the proper organization, you can keep the employee hunt from turning into a fiasco.

First, the object is to match the applicant to the job, not vice versa. So you'll have to look at a number of applicants. How do

15

you find these people? Here are a few ways of searching for potential employees:

- Employment agencies, public and private.
- Advertising for employees.
- Recruiting from schools—high schools, two-year colleges, four-year colleges, trade schools.
- Labor unions and other specialized organizations.
- Employee referrals.
- Walk-ins.
- Recruiting from competitors.
- Recruiting from organizations for the handicapped or disadvantaged.
- Recruiting minorities.
- Situation-wanted ads.
- Temporary employment agencies.
- Family.

As you can see, you have a great deal to work with, but decide which of these techniques will work for you. Let's take each method of obtaining new employees and see which strikes your fancy.

EMPLOYMENT AGENCIES

Often an owner will pick up the phone and call an agency. There are two basic types to choose from—public, government-sponsored agencies and private agencies run as businesses (most of them small businesses themselves).

The public agencies are primarily useful in finding people for lower-level and blue-collar jobs. In the past, the public agencies had a bad (and deserved) reputation. In fact, they were known as "unemployment agencies," because many of their clients were interested in remaining unemployed and collecting welfare or unemployment compensation, not in finding jobs. But some states have excellent agencies which operate efficiently. These agencies are free and provide many employment services, such as employment testing.

The alternative to the public employment agency is the private employment agency. Private agencies run the gamut. Some are gigantic coast-to-coast operations placing thousands of people. Others are tiny businesses run out of private homes. Some specialize, while others will try to place any kind of employee. Most important, some agencies are solid, helpful businesses and others are fly-by-night rip-offs. It pays to know which is which.

Private agencies make money by charging a fee. Most of the time you'll pay the fee if you hire one of their clients. In some cases, the applicant pays the agency's fee.

A good private agency will utilize the information you supply, advertise, and screen applicants for the job—ending up by sending you the cream of the crop. It's a real service with measured results. But the best agency must work with the information you supply. If you are hazy in your instructions or supply an inadequate job description, don't expect the agency to perform miracles.

Another problem small business owners face is the inability to make decisions. Often they'll supply the agency with a job description and leave the hiring to them by taking the first applicant the agency sends over. This isn't profitable in most cases. You are part of the hiring process—it's your business, and no one understands it better than you. You must rely upon yourself to make the important decisions. Never let an agency cow you, or overwhelm you with jargon; if they try, get another agency.

So employment agencies can be an excellent source of good people—if you keep a strong hand in the selection process.

ADVERTISING

Advertising for employees is not as simple as it seems. Before you advertise you need to know where to advertise, how to advertise, how to write the ad, and how to handle the responses.

The first step is to write the ad. Some small businessmen use a copy of the job summary for the ad. But you need to do more than that for maximum results. Think of the ad as a selling device—you want to sell the job and your company, and attract the best people to the job. You need to make them notice you above your competition. This doesn't mean you have to go overboard and use Madison Avenue cereal-advertising techniques, but it does mean that your ad should be interesting.

Too many ads don't tell you anything:

Buyer, midtown location.
Call Bonnie at . . .

This ad will attract responses in a tight job market, but not as well as this ad which followed it:

BUYER, Lingerie
Bright future with exciting, fast-paced young company. Position in metropolitan area. Want an aggressive, experienced pro, min. 2 yrs. Top dollar for right person. Send resume and covering letter to . . .

This advertisement sells the job a little better. It also tells the potential applicant the type of work and the kind of person the company wants, eliminating many unqualified responses.

If you are really interested in drawing a maximum of responses, you can use different sizes of type, boxed ads, more white space. An ad that jumps off the page at the reader naturally will pull in more responses. Some advertisers are still using such old chestnuts as heading the ad with a word like SEX! in large type, then continuing with "now that I've got your attention . . ."

It's up to you, but basically the ad must:

• Be clear.
• Be interesting.
• Be specific.
• Portray the type of employee you want—list requirements.
• Explain how you want the applicants to respond.

The next step is placing your ad. Who do you want to read it? You have many alternatives. You can place your ad in a daily newspaper, or wait until Sunday and utilize the larger classified section, or advertise in a weekly handout, or place the ad in a trade journal or specialized publication.

The only problem with journals is that they are published monthly. Daily and Sunday papers present a different problem. You'll have no problem receiving responses—on the contrary, you may be overwhelmed. This is why some owners prefer to use private agencies. All responses are directed to the agency, so the headache is theirs.

One way to protect yourself from a rush of applicants beating at your doors is to write a blind ad—one that gives a box number to respond to. The applicants write to the box number and you decide which applicants you want to interview. On the other hand, if your business is in a small town or an area where labor is in demand, you'll probably want to use a signed ad—one in which your business is identified.

But whether the labor market is tight or not, the ad should be a selling tool to draw the best people to your business.

SCHOOLS

Keep in mind who you want. Don't try to recruit from a college or university if you don't have an upper-level entry job to offer. Colleges and universities are fine for supplying managerial trainees or highly trained personnel, such as chemists.

Community colleges and trade schools can be excellent sources for technicians or skilled business workers. For example, if you need a computer operator or a lab technician, you should try one of these schools. You won't get an experienced worker, but you will get a well-trained one. Don't forget vocational schools if you need a mechanic or a hairdresser. You'll have to train these people a little more than experienced workers, but it may be worth it.

High schools also are good sources of trainee-level personnel. More students than ever are taking business or trade courses in high school in preparation for full-time jobs after graduation.

You should contact the guidance or career offices in all of these schools. They can put you in immediate touch with interested students.

Don't forget who you are hiring, if you do hire from a school, whether it's a college or high school. You are hiring a beginner—someone with all the basics but no experience. Someone you'll have to watch carefully. This arrangement can turn out to be excellent: The starting salary will be less for an inexperienced worker, and you'll have a clean slate to work on. But don't make the mistake of bringing the new employee along too quickly. The orientation for this type of employee has to be especially smooth. (See discussion of orientation in Part II.)

LABOR UNIONS AND ORGANIZATIONS

If your business has a union, chances are you'll check the union offices first. Unions have enlisted a sizable chunk of personnel in the United States.

If you need a specialized worker, you can contact an association or society. For example, if you need a chemist you can check with the clearing offices of the American Chemical Society. Such organizations are always interested in placing their members.

EMPLOYEE REFERRALS

Ask a good employee where to find others. Many times they'll have someone in mind. But be careful, you're treading on thin ice here. If you decide not to hire the person they suggested or hire a recommended person who doesn't work out, you may lose your good employee along with the recommended one.

WALK-INS

Walk-ins are people who walk in off the street or apply on their own in some way. Obviously, walk-ins aren't a reliable recruiting source. Usually you'll have no need for them—at the time they apply. It is not bad policy to take a few minutes, have them fill out an application, and talk to them. Sometimes a job opens up unexpectedly and a walk-in may offer the best choice. Some employers like walk-ins because they have the initiative to contact the employer on their own.

RECRUITING FROM COMPETITORS

This is a sticky area. If you spot a really good employee who is working for your biggest competitor, there are three points to consider:

- Would that employee help my business?
- Would hiring that worker hurt my competitor?
- Can you afford to start an employee war?

First, whatever you do, do it aboveboard. Approach both the competitor and the employee. Your competitor may be delighted to help you out and give his employee a chance at a better job. On the other hand, your competitor may be enraged. If that's the case, you have a decision to make. Hire away and start a range war, or forget it and remain friendly competitors.

ORGANIZATIONS FOR THE HANDICAPPED OR DISADVANTAGED

Many jobs in American industry do not require all the senses. Bob discovered this when he decided to hire a blind man to assemble radio components in his small plant. The initial training period was more intense than most, and some changes had to be made at the new employee's working station, but Bob discovered that he had hired an excellent and gifted employee.

The same applies to the mentally handicapped, physically disabled, and disadvantaged groups such as ex-convicts. Many will be good employees when given the chance. Contact a local organization representing these groups. You may discover a potentially excellent source of good people.

MINORITIES

It's good business to hire from minority groups. You may have to invest more time in the training period, but the results can be worthwhile. Get in touch with local organizations, church and social associations.

SITUATION-WANTED ADS

These are ads placed by individuals looking for a job. Many employers like them because they cost the company no money. If you see a situation-wanted ad which lists qualifications you like, all it costs you is some time on the phone or a letter to check out the person.

TEMPORARY EMPLOYMENT AGENCIES

At times, your business may be swamped with work. You need more employees, but you know this rush will last only a few days or weeks. You certainly don't want to go through the rigors of hiring employees and then firing them in a short time. The alternative is working with a temporary help service. Figure out your needs, contact the agency, and they'll send you employees. They also take care of the worker's salary, social security, etc. All you do is pay a flat hourly fee to the agency.

Working with a temporary agency is similar to working with any private agency—in fact, many agencies do both full-time and temporary supplying. So pick the agency carefully—shop around. And don't forget to supply all the pertinent information in order to get the employees you want.

FAMILY AND RELATIVES

The best is saved for last. Sooner or later you'll probably have to handle this problem—although sometimes it isn't really a problem at all. Everyone is familiar with the horror stories about how the no-good son destroyed a profitable business built from scratch by the self-sacrificing, hard-working father. Then there's the nephew, niece, or second cousin your family has been pushing down your throat. "Why he's your own flesh and blood! You have to hire poor Sidney."

It is a difficult situation—if the relative is a pariah. You have to choose between taking on deadwood and shutting him or her away in the basement counting widgets, or incurring the wrath of your family.

But there are many times a relative is a good choice. There's less chance that a relative will steal you blind or sell secrets to a competitor. He or she may take more than ordinary interest in building your business.

All the same, if you can't afford to hire a relative, don't. It's better to face down your family than cripple your business.

Now that you have a few ways of hunting the perfect employee, go on to the next step: pinpointing the applicant.

THREE

Handling Applicants

The Interview / Checking References / Testing

NOW THAT YOU HAVE A MULTITUDE OF WARM BODIES applying, what do you do? Find out as much as you can about them. No matter if the job is an important, prestigious one, such as assistant manager, or a lower-level entry position, such as cash register operator or dishwasher, you still need to know important basic facts.

First, have all applicants fill out an application form, a valuable tool for big or small business. It is merely a starting point in your quest for information about the applicant, and gives you some basic facts which will later be supplemented by an interview.

Generally, small businesses use simplified application forms which ask questions relating to previous employment, education, personal information, etc. The application form can be short and simple. You can buy one commercially or make up your own. It can be a Xeroxed or mimeographed typed page.

What you want to know about the applicants are facts which relate to their performance on the job. Some years ago, businesses felt that they had a right to pry into every facet of their employees' existence. "Do you smoke in bed? Have you always been faithful to your husband or wife? Have you ever considered smoking pot? Have you ever been arrested?" Employers felt these questions would give them true insight into the moral

SAMPLE APPLICATION FORM

Name _____Date _____
      (last)   (first)   (middle)

Address _____Phone no. _____
Date of birth _____Height _____Weight _____
Place of birth _____U.S. citizen? _____
Single ____Married ____Divorced ____Widowed ____Separated____
Social Security no. _____No. of dependents _____
Health: Good _____Fair _____Poor _____
List handicaps, chronic ailments, serious illnesses: _____
_____
Person to notify in case of accident _____
Address _____Phone no. _____
Minimum salary expected _____

Education

	(name and address)	(from)	(to)	(graduated)
Elementary				
High school				
College				
Other				

Experience

(list last employer first)	(dates)	(job)	(reason for leaving)
Firm _____	From		
Address _____			
Supervisor_____	To		
Firm _____	From		
Address _____			
Supervisor_____	To		
Firm _____	From		
Address _____			
Supervisor_____	To		

fiber of applicants. A good employee had to be an upright member of the community and salute the American flag twice a day.

There now exists a thin line between trying to uncover important facts and unnecessary prying into private affairs. Certainly you need to know how dependable a potential employee will be. If he or she is going to pillage your business, walk out in the middle of a shift, never show up on time, or beat up other workers, you'd naturally like to know about it. But the application form can reveal only so much; it is a first step in the discovery process.

Also, there are questions you can't, according to law, ask on the application form. For example, questions which ask religious affiliation. You can't have a blank next to "Religion" on the form—and the same with race and national origin. If you stick to information that is strictly business-related, you'll be in compliance with employment laws.

The completed application form tells you several things about the applicant. First, it reveals answers to the questions on the form. But it also shows if an applicant can follow instructions. In this day and age of high school graduates with third-grade educations, it helps to know if the applicant can read, write, and comprehend.

After you read the completed application form, you should know whether or not the applicant fills the minimal job requirements—the qualifications you determined after you analyzed the job. If the answer is no, you've eliminated one applicant. If the answer is yes, you're ready for the next step—the interview.

THE INTERVIEW

There has been some question in the past about the importance of an interview in the hiring process. To interviewers who were aspiring psychologists, the interview was all-important—the tool to probe the applicant's soul. At the other end of the scale were the detractors who felt the interview was of very limited value. They felt that there were too many ways an applicant could take advantage of the interviewer and skillfully give wrong impressions. Solid, traceable facts supplied by the application form were felt to be more important.

Actually, an interview can be an excellent tool or a waste of time. It all depends on the interviewer. This is a serious problem with many small business owners. They rarely know how to interview, which is understandable. Large and middle-sized companies have personnel staffs to screen applicants. The small business owner doesn't. He or she is in an uncomfortable, unfamiliar position.

First, what can the interview accomplish for you?

- It gives you the opportunity to meet the applicant face to face.
- It gives you the opportunity to discover more information.
- It allows you to tell the applicant more about the job and your business.
- It allows you to see if the real person lives up to his or her advance billing.

There are certain important steps before you begin the interview. First, be prepared. Go over the application form. Prepare a list of questions. Keep a checklist to use during the interview. Pay careful attention to every word. A checklist with categories such as speech, dress, attitude, allows you to make a simple mark in the appropriate box. The interview isn't disrupted.

In addition to preparing questions, prepare yourself. The interview is your first contact in the job process with a living, breathing human being. Before the interview, the applicant was a few written lines on an application form. Now you must deal with a person.

It isn't easy. You have to keep a part of yourself uninvolved while another part is trying to make friends and really understand the applicant. For example, a very tall man—6'6"—walks in to be interviewed. Immediately, you say to yourself, "Wow, the guy's so tall he must be good." You can't afford to be overwhelmed by the applicant's physical characteristics, unless they are relevant to job performance. And don't fall for the Elizabeth Ray syndrome, where the interview is conducted something like this:

Interviewer: Can you type?
Beautiful Blonde: Fifteen words a minute.
Int.: That's good. Can you take shorthand?
B.B.: Short what?
Int.: You start Monday.

Your business can't afford this. So don't allow yourself to be drawn away from the real purpose of the interview.

Before the applicant opens his or her mouth, there are two things you will discover—even if you're far from a Sherlock Holmes.

- *Promptness:* Was the applicant on time for the interview? A person who cares about the job should be prompt.
- *Personal appearance:* Was he or she neat and well groomed or unkempt and sloppy?

A small restaurant owner interviewed applicants for a waiter's job. One individual smelled like a football locker room. No matter what this man did throughout the rest of the interview, he had lost the job before he opened his mouth. Of course you don't expect an applicant for a warehouse job to be dressed in a Brooks Brothers suit, but you can expect a neat appearance.

You've introduced yourself and the applicant is asked to sit down. The interview is about to begin. Before you start firing questions, try to make the applicant at ease. This is vital. You need crisp, clear answers to your questions. You don't want the applicant freezing up. Remember that you are on your own home ground during the interview. The applicant has just made a trek into unknown territory. Also, you are the person who will make a decision about the applicant's future. You have the almighty power of yes or no. Can you blame the applicant for being nervous?

Interviews are a source of extreme torture for some people. One woman looking for a job in social services couldn't sleep the night before the interview, couldn't eat, and became physically ill. Yet she was highly skilled, capable, and dependable.

So make the applicant feel at home. Be a sympathetic friend. Try to find common ground and chew the fat for a few minutes. What you need to do is draw the person out, trying to discover what he or she is really like. Your business is small and you'll have to work in close contact with anyone you hire. So try to get a feeling about what the applicant would be like to work with. It should be a major goal throughout the entire interview.

Another major purpose of the interview is to uncover more in-depth information about the applicant. The interview is another stepping stone toward understanding the person. You need to know:

- How the applicant will perform on the job.
- How the applicant will relate to other workers.
- How the applicant will fit into the company.
- What future aspirations the applicant has.

To discover all you want to know about the applicant, you must know what questions to ask and how to listen. You have to control the interview, but you can't dominate it. The applicant must be free to answer all your questions. In turn, answer questions about your business.

Ronald was interviewing applicants for administrative assistant. Throughout the interview with Marcia, he was friendly and asked questions that demanded full responses. Then he asked Marcia what her future plans were. He was stunned to discover her telling him an involved story about how she only planned to work a few months, long enough to make the amount of money she needed to cut a demonstration record. Then she was going to fly off to Nashville and take a crack at being a music personality. By this point in the interview they were great friends. After the interview Marcia felt pleased with the way things went. So did Ronald. He knew that there was not a chance in the world that he was going to hire a temporary administrative assistant.

A big problem with too many interviewers is that they engage in an unnecessary hard sell of the business. They use the interview as a sounding board and launch into involved spiels. At the end of the interview, the talkative ones will discover thay have just a few thin impressions of the applicant and no new facts. So although the interview is a two-way street, the traffic from the applicant should be heavier. It's more important that you discover new information about a potential employee than that you engage in an annual report.

Interview more than one or two applicants. It's important that you get a balanced view of the caliber of employees available. The first two may look good, but the third and fourth applicants may be out of this world.

You may also want to get the opinion of someone you trust who already works for you. One of your goals is to select an individual who will get along with your existing employees. So let one of your trusted employees also interview the applicants.

There is one pitfall you want to avoid—your second interviewer must have the best interests of the company at heart. Dan had his assistant manager interview all the applicants for a newly created administrative assistant position. Dan was surprised to find that his assistant manager had eliminated all college graduates from consideration. It turned out that the assistant manager, who had only completed two years of college, was afraid of competition for his own job. From that time on, Dan did the interviewing on his own.

A second opinion is always good, whether in medicine or business. But since you are in charge, the ultimate decision is yours alone.

Let's sum up what makes a good interview:

- Preparing questions and checklists in advance.
- Putting the applicant at ease.
- Guiding the interview but not overwhelming it.
- Listening—THIS IS IMPORTANT!
- Asking questions that draw out the applicant.
- Evaluating the interview while it is still fresh in your mind.

The last point is important. When it comes time to make a choice, don't be guided by fuzzy impressions. Write an evaluation of the applicant the minute the interview terminates.

When the interview ends, it is important to be just as kind to the applicant as you were during the interview. This person is still in the dark. Was the interview a success or a dismal failure? The best you can do is tell the applicant that he or she will be informed of the decision in a few days. This should be your response whether or not you plan to hire the person. Never humiliate someone at the end of an interview by saying, "Sorry, but I'm afraid you just aren't the type for us." All further correspondence should be by mail or telephone. If your answer is no, make it a positive no and an easy letdown.

CHECKING REFERENCES

After the interview is over and you have the application form filled out, you have a big job in front of you: Does all that information check out? Everything needs to be verified. The *New York Times* recently ran a story about a young man who applied to and was accepted by Yale. Yale had taken one look at the young man's transcripts and application and felt certain that they had discovered a genius. The man had written that he had a perfect academic record in high school, but had taken a few years off to amass a tremendous fortune in business. Yale swallowed the story hook, line, and sinker. Of course the man's background was faked. And Yale never would have discovered that fact, except that the man became bored with school and spilled the beans.

Yale is a university, and the man did little harm wandering around the hallowed halls (except to the school's ego). But transfer his case to the business world. A person with every skill and qualification you need applies for the job opening. His credentials are impressive. You are tempted to hire him on the spot. Don't! Check carefully first. What if you do hire him, say as assistant manager. He's an absolute gem for the first week. Then one morning you discover that he's gone—and so are the cash receipts.

Certainly, this is an extreme example. Many people who falsify information simply lack experience. Sure, in the movies or on TV, the person who lies to get a job is really so extraordinary that by the time the boss has discovered the lie, the culprit is already his son-in-law and sitting on the board of directors. Real life is different. It's frustrating to find that Berlin Wall of "experience only" blocking your way, when you don't have any. So what's the harm of a little white lie? Not much to the person applying for the job, but what about the small business owner? He or she takes the chance of hiring someone who can't do the job—or someone who is a habitual crook.

How do you verify information supplied to you? The first step is to make sure that all the information is factual. Did Susan really attend Valley View High School, did she spend a year at Sunnyside College, did she work for six months as a typist at Bowles & Co.? The object of this type of search is to check the black-and-white statements. If the applicant did indeed do exactly as she said, you've made a good start. The applicant isn't a liar.

The next step is more difficult. How did the applicant perform at previous jobs? Why was he or she discharged? These answers may not be easy to get. Many former bosses aren't eager to give detrimental information which will jeopardize someone's chance at another job. And there have been cases where former bosses have been sued for giving information which undeservedly ruined a former employee's ability to find a job. But the former employer can tell you the exact reasons for dismissal—especially if it was criminal behavior.

The best method of checking is by using the phone or meeting with the former boss face to face. You can get more of a feeling about the impression the employee made. And, of course, there's nothing in writing to indict the former boss.

Checking an employee is demanding work. You have to be on your toes at all times. Former bosses aren't always fair. A former boss may have been the reason an employee quit. So remember, there are two sides to every story. If, during the interview, the applicant told of being harassed on his previous job by a foreman who just didn't like him, dig into that during the phone check. The information may just verify the applicant's story.

At this point, you have checked and rechecked all the pertinent information. Many applicants have been eliminated for one reason or another. You're left with a handful of the best. It's time to proceed to the next level.

TESTING

To test or not to test is sometimes the question. Are tests valuable? Like everything else, tests are praised and cursed. But most of the praise is from large companies that can afford batteries of tests and trained psychologists to interpret test results.

There are plenty of tests to choose from. Complete test packages can be bought by any small business—but are they worth the expense? It depends on how and what you want to test. If you want to hire a secretary or a bartender, there is little reason to give the applicants an I.Q. test. On the other hand, a demonstration showing a secretary's or bartender's skill might be appropriate. This type of test is easy to make up and administer—and the results are easy to interpret. Say you want to see if an applicant will make a good bartender. Simply watch. If the applicant can make a good gin fizz and a terrific Singapore Sling, it will show. You can add some pressure to a simple test like this. Give the aspiring bartender a list of five drinks and time how long it takes to make the drinks. While the drinks are being made, talk to the bartender, try to distract him or her, engage in real-life situations and see how the applicant stands up to the pressure.

Tests that measure skills are fine as long as the skills are measurable. But what if you want to hire an assistant manager? The manager's skills aren't easily tested in a simple demonstration. Sure, you can submit the applicants to all sorts of psychological tests, but most small businesses can't interpret results or afford a psychologist to do the interpreting.

So tests have limited value. Be careful before you decide to submit applicants to testing. The results can be misleading. And even a perfect test isn't a foolproof means of selection. The test is only one segment of the hiring process. You have to weigh any test results with every other piece of information about the applicant.

There is one test that should be given, however—a physical examination. It should be given great attention if the job is physically demanding or stressful. A man with a slipped disc shouldn't be hired for the loading dock—no matter if he's crazy enough to apply for the job.

There are other reasons for administering a physical examination. You comply with workman's compensation laws by having a record of the employee's health when he or she enters the job. Also, if the physician detects something wrong with the employee, you have a record of it—there won't be a chance for work-induced injury claims from old wounds.

It is good procedure to complete the exam before the applicant is hired. If, for any reason, the physical exam turns up cause for alarm, it's better to know before the person is hired. Let's assume you've agreed to hire a person who has quit another job, even moved to a better location. Then out of the blue, the physical causes him or her to lose the new job. There's always the chance that the physical exam results will be vital. So know about it in advance.

Since small businesses can't afford company doctors, the best procedure is to use a local doctor. Choose the doctor carefully, then send all your prospective employees to that same doctor.

FOUR

Equal Opportunity Employment

TODAY, ATTITUDES AND ROLES ARE DIFFERENT FROM twenty, even ten years ago. For example, Marge, a young woman of twenty, decided to apply for the position of forklift trainee in a small factory. The owner took one look at her, placed a fatherly arm around her shoulders, and told her she would be better off looking for a job as a secretary and a good man for a husband. Marge was humiliated and very enraged. The factory had twenty-five employees and was covered by Title VII of the Civil Rights Act. Marge filed suit, charging sex discrimination against the factory. She won a cash victory. The shocked owner learned a costly lesson.

Not all owners are as blunt as this factory owner. They'll accept any applicant, but always hire the "type" they had in mind beforehand. If you have set ideas about race, sex, age, or physical stature, reconsider. By limiting yourself to one group, you are cutting down your options for many excellent employees. There is no reason a woman can't handle a forklift. The same goes for any other group. Open your mind to new possibilities.

Jack ran a small manufacturing plant with ten employees. His business was located in a part of town that was predominately black, but Jack had no black employees. Jack was a small fish. Title VII didn't apply to him, because he had fewer than fifteen employees and no federal contracts. So Jack felt very secure. He had no black employees because he didn't want any black employees, which he felt was his own business. But one day Jack found he did have a few problems. Local community leaders got tired of the situation at Jack's plant. Not only was Jack located in the black community, he also did most of his business there, supplying many black-owned businesses. The final result was a boycott by black business owners. A suit was brought against him by the State's Human Rights Commission, which in most states can take cases involving fewer than fifteen employees. In the end, Jack lost the lion's share of his business and got a lot of bad publicity, all because of his irrational bigoted attitude.

The point is that small business owners are not exempt from anti-discrimination laws. It's just that small businesses can get away with a great deal of blatant discrimination because there are so many bigger fish to fry in the business world. There are plenty of small business owners who don't hire women, blacks, Jews, Hispanics, American Indians, Eastern Europeans, Orientals, etc.—there are regional variations on the same theme. In fact, the pendulum has swung back, because now white males are claiming discrimination—WASP males are now a minority group!

It's a big mistake to discriminate on the basis of race, religion, sex, or age. You're only hurting yourself by these exclusionary acts. There are many "reasons" given for discrimination. Some owners claim they don't consider themselves prejudiced—they hang the blame on their customers. Sherry, who owned a beauty salon, refused to hire female hair stylists. She claimed that her customers preferred to have a man do their hair. Paul, owner of a real estate agency, refused to hire blacks, Chicanos, or Orientals. He claimed that his customers would be offended and ill at ease—especially if they wanted to confide in an agent that they were interested in white-only communities.

This game is an easy one to play, and it helps soothe consciences. Both Sherry and Paul have invented perfect rationalizations—business would suffer if they gave in to their own unbiased tendencies. The fact is that they *are* discriminating, and being unfair to themselves and their customers. Most women don't give a damn who does their hair, as long as the stylist is competent. And in the real estate business, it's dangerous to discriminate in housing, so hiring minorities shouldn't make any difference.

You can almost hear many business people saying, "But that's the way things are. You can't ignore hard business facts—the customer is picky about the people you hire." Well, that's not the way things are in the vast majority of cases. Both your business and the community suffer if you persist in discrimination.

No business can afford to hire nonproductive employees. Apply the same standards to all employees. It doesn't matter if the applicant is male or female, black or white, Catholic or Buddhist. Your business needs the best you can get. If a reference check turns up a serious police record, think twice before you turn your business into a rehabilitation center. It's risky and you'd be a fool to do it. Or if the applicant was dismissed from the last job because of theft, there's no way you should hire that individual.

Adopt a fair policy in hiring and stick to it. Sure, you can discriminate if you want and you'll probably get away with it. But it's narrow-minded and unprofitable. The true qualifier is not sex or race or age, but whether or not the applicant can do the job better than all other applicants.

FIVE

The Final Selection

YOU'RE AT THE POINT IN THE SELECTION PROCESS WHERE you're ready to make a decision. You have a number of likely candidates for the job—all of them, hopefully, solid types who can help your business. Which one will you pick?

If you've done your homework, you should know all you need to know about the applicants. Now you make your choice. Of course, that's easier said than done. Even with all the precautions you've taken, hiring is still a gamble. No one knows the future. But you've interviewed, checked and rechecked all the best people.

Again, as in interviewing, you may want to ask the opinion of your employees and weigh their comments or observations. But the choice is yours. How do the candidates stack up? Records, forms, interviews, impressions, reference checks with former employers—are all elements that have to be considered.

After you have selected your future employee, don't dump the records of the rest of the applicants in the wastebasket. There are many unforeseen problems that can crop up between the time of selection, the applicant's acceptance of the job, and the smooth adjustment of the new employee into your work force. For example, your first choice might not accept the job offer. Or your first choice may not work out during the probationary period. That's where the other applicants come in. If number one doesn't work, maybe number two, three, or four will. As they say in a beauty contest: If for any reason the winner can't serve, the first runner-up assumes the title.

So when you accept one applicant, don't burn your records behind you. When informing applicants you didn't select, be diplomatic. Write to them and let them know exactly where they stand as soon as possible. And if there is a chance that they will be considered for a future opening, let them know.

Here's a sample rejection letter:

Dear Mr. Smith:

Although you have impressive credentials for the job, I regret to inform you that you were not selected for the position. Someone who even more closely fitted our requirements was hired.

We will keep your name (resume) on file if we have a future opening in your line. Thank you very much for your interest in our business.

Even if you don't want one of the applicants under any circumstances, it pays to be polite. It costs you very little. And always let all the applicants know of your decision. After an interview and a pep talk from the interviewer, an applicant may go away with high hopes for the job. He or she may hang around the phone or mailbox for a couple of weeks waiting for a sign from you. Finally the applicant will call, only to be informed that the position was filled last week. That's poor practice. Drop a line quickly to let them know they should continue their job search.

So much for losers. You also have to be careful with the person you plan to hire. You want that person. Be friendly and open in your letter or phone call. Congratulate him or her. This is the beginning of the induction process. Whether you're hiring a dishwasher or a district manager, you want a well-adjusted, productive worker.

Whether you inform the individual by phone or letter, make sure that you both have the same job in mind. Sally was overjoyed when the advertising agency called her and told her the job was hers. She had applied for an account-executive trainee position. But when she reported for the first day of work, she discovered that the agency had hired her as a secretary. The agency had already filled the trainee spot and felt that Sally would make a good secretary. Unfortunately, they hadn't mentioned the change to her, and she quit ten minutes later.

Also clear up such matters as salary, vacation time, benefits, hours worked, and any other pertinent conditions. Be sure you and your future employee are in agreement on these before beginning work. It saves a lot of future hassles.

You've made your selection, and in a day, a week, or whenever, the new employee will be reporting to his or her job. You've taken a big first step, but your work is far from over. In many ways it is just beginning.

Part II

ORIENTATION AND TRAINING

SIX

The First Few Days

Start with a Clean Slate / Step by Step

Y OU'VE HIRED SOMEONE. BRIGHT AND EARLY MONDAY
morning, he or she will walk into a new job. You, as owner
and boss, can make that new job look mighty good or mighty
bad. Put yourself in your new employee's shoes. Look back to
when you started a new job. How did you feel? Excited, yes, but
also nervous, anxious to make a good impression, unsure of
yourself, afraid to offend, worried about your co-workers—and
you probably tried to hide all of these feelings beneath a thin
veneer of aggressiveness or tranquility.

A job isn't just a nine-to-five "stack those boxes, type that
letter" existence. A job is a big chunk of a person's life. And
people need more than money from a job. They need to feel
worthwhile. It's up to you to provide a helping hand and support to the new employee—to make the new job pleasant and exciting instead of dull and dispiriting.

The new employee doesn't know what to expect the moment
he or she walks through the front door. Sure, the person was
probably introduced to your other employees. And the new employee knows a little bit about what the job is all about. But
that's it. The new employee is a babe in the wilderness, wonder-
ing about the heart and soul—the guts—of the job. What makes
it tick? Are the other employees easy to work with, or is everyone out to stab unprotected backs? And what about the boss?

How good a manager? How strict? Will the boss listen to problems? Will he or she listen to a new employee, or do you have to work for the business at least five years?

The new employee should be eased into the job and the company the same way you ease yourself into a hot tub: slowly, acclimatizing each part of your body. By the time the new employee is all the way in, he or she should be as comfortable as you are in your bath.

All new employees need a period of grace, no matter how experienced they are at their work. Your company has a whole new set of rules. It's a different ballgame.

It's easy to discover whether you have a proper orientation program. Take a look at turnover statistics. What percentage of employees quit or are discharged within a few weeks? If it is a large percentage, you had better remodel your program, if you had one at all. It doesn't pay to throw new employees to the wolves.

Dale discovered this in his country club. Every summer he had to hire four or five people to work the short-order stand by the pool. He always started the new employee on a weekday. The person was given a couple of instructions, like where the food was and where the grill was, and that was it. During the first week there were a few little problems, but things usually went smoothly enough. But on weekends the country club was mobbed—therefore the counter was mobbed. The poor, unsuspecting employee was swamped. After a couple of weeks with no help or encouragement from Dale, the new employee quit. It was just a case of being thrown to a horde of hungry club members—worse than wolves.

START WITH A CLEAN SLATE

When your new employee arrives for work the first time, start with a clean slate. Consider what you want to get across to this new employee. First, you want to acquaint him or her with all the duties of the job. Second, you want to establish the rules and regulations of your business. Third, you'll want to outline all the pertinent information about your business—its history, its importance, who you do business with, what functions you serve, etc. How do you get all of this through to the new employee?

Most small businesses let it take care of itself. The owners deal with the questions as they come up—and they usually don't worry about it if their employees don't have the "big picture" of their business.

There is a better way. Use an employee handbook. This is an excellent orientation tool. It should contain everything you want your employees to know. A sample table of contents from the SBA's booklet, "Pointers on Preparing an Employee Handbook," is given on page 48. Your business probably won't need such a thorough handbook, but it does give you an idea about how to set up your own handbook.

Your employee handbook doesn't have to be a hard-cover masterpiece. A couple of typed pages, Xeroxed and stapled, will be fine. It's the information that counts. It should be written clearly and to the point. Don't confuse your employees and yourself by hiring a lawyer to write it.

The employee handbook is not a means of eliminating personal contact. If an employee comes to you with a question, don't reply that the answer is in the handbook. It is a supplement and a guide—not the last word in employee instruction.

If your business is a complex one and you feel that a more intense method of induction is necessary, you can invest in an inexpensive slide show. Ken owned a small plant that manufactured special drilling equipment. He had an audiovisual company create a slide show for new employees. It included a series of slides and a cassette recording that explored the different steps in manufacturing and the importance of the equipment to the drilling industry. The entire presentation took fifteen minutes, and by the time it was over, the new employee had a good view of the company. Ken had professionals do his show. The investment was substantial in comparison to two typed sheets of information, but the results were worth the cost.

You don't necessarily need an expensive slide or film presentation. If you're handy with a camera, you can work up a slide show or some other sort of visual presentation. Just remember to keep it clear, to the point, and interesting.

Employee Handbook:
SAMPLE TABLE OF CONTENTS

What you are doing with these presentations to new employees is infusing your business—and by extension, their jobs—with a sense of meaning. The new employee is getting an overall look, and he or she is discovering his or her place in the company. It helps a new employee feel at home.

STEP BY STEP

Your goal as manager is to turn the new employee into an efficient worker. This means that the new employee will have to be trained. Now, *training* is an all-inclusive word. If your new employee is a dishwasher, the training program will probably last half an hour or so. On the other hand, if you are hiring an apprentice plumber, the training program will last several years.

Before you can train anyone, you must go back to the first step, the job analysis (Chapter One). You must know everything you can about the job. It seems obvious, but many small business owners waste time, money, and employee patience in what they think is a training program, because they haven't really analyzed the job. The old adage, "Those who can, do; those can't, teach" better not apply to your business. You can't afford to waste your training period.

Dig deeply into the job. Take it step by step, and go over those steps with your employee. But you yourself have to know what the job is all about. Charles got into serious trouble because he didn't. Charles ran a small public relations and consulting firm. For six years he had gathered new accounts and kept the steady clients happy—he was a very good salesman. He could pull in double the business his small company could handle. But behind the scenes was Roy. Roy organized meetings, wrote the brochures, press releases, and annual reports—he headed the entire productive operation of the company.

One day Roy got a better job offer and quit. At first Charles wasn't worried. He hadn't been getting along too well with Roy recently. He even told Roy he didn't have to stick around to help break in a new person to replace him. After all, there were three assistant writers. Charles believed that all he had to do was promote one of them into Roy's position, and he could go back to lunches with clients.

Charles had forgotten the complexities of Roy's job. Roy was more than a writer, he was also a terrific coordinator who understood the ins and outs of Charles' business. All Charles knew was that deadlines were met and business meetings and presentations went smoothly. The clients were happy, so Charles was happy.

After two weeks without Roy, Charles suddenly discovered that things were going haywire. The new production head was swamped. He came to Charles several times to ask about procedures, but all he got was an icy glare and a curt "That's your part of the business. It's up to you to figure things out." Meetings were mixed up, assignments weren't completed, deadlines were forgotten, writers and artists were at each other's throats—and worst of all, clients were pulling up stakes.

All this happened because Charles was a prima donna who didn't understand his own business. It was his responsibility to pitch in and train the promoted employee, help him over the rough spots. Then his business wouldn't have been thrown into chaos. Charles' predicament also underscores another small business adage: Never trust your business operations to one key employee. Illness, death, quarrels, job offers could all play havoc with your livelihood.

Therefore, know all the job functions. You can't expect an employee to be a miracle worker. You have to communicate this to the employee too, or your job analysis is worthless.

Ed ran a pet store. He hired Mary Beth as a cashier. Now Ed knew that he wanted his new employee to do more than sit at the cash register, but he never told Mary Beth. On her first day she found out. Ed asked her to straighten the back room. By the middle of the second day, Mary Beth discovered that her duties included cleaning, window displays, arrangements, feeding the fish, and general odd jobs when she wasn't needed at the cash register. After all, it was a small store and she couldn't just sit at the cash register waiting for customers.

On the third day, Ed handed Mary Beth a pair of gloves and said that it was time to feed the snakes. When she asked Ed to show her the snake food and he pointed to a mouse cage—that was it. The next thing Ed knew, he was holding the gloves and watching Mary Beth disappear out the front door.

No matter how logical the work seems to you, you can't give an employee his or her duties piecemeal. The job description adds the clause "any task the employer wants done." This is to protect you from the employee who follows the job description to the letter. But you can't abuse it. If you continue to call on an employee to do every little job you seem to pick out of the blue, all you're doing is disrupting and confusing the worker. Ed did it that way and lost an excellent employee.

The orientation period is a time in which the employee becomes familiarized with his or her duties. It also is the time you become familiarized with your new employee. Small business owners usually don't have to worry about not seeing enough of their employees. But with a new employee, you have to see and understand. For the first few weeks keep in constant touch. This shouldn't be too hard, because you'll probably be supervising the training. But if the training lasts a couple of days, make an effort to be available. It could save you the bother of looking for another employee.

What should any orientation and induction period accomplish?

- Teach the new employee company rules and regulations.
- Familiarize the new employee with *all* aspects of the job.
- Familiarize the employee with the company.
- Help the employee to become part of the business.

The next step after induction is training.

SEVEN

The Training Phase

*Checklist for Developing a Training Program / Selecting
the Trainer / Training Upper-Level Personnel*

ALL NEW EMPLOYEES NEED TRAINING, WHETHER THE training is a few hours of instruction or a rigid three-month program. Before you plunge into the training of a new employee, or the retraining of an old employee, be sure that you are prepared. You, the owner, have to be just as prepared as the trainees. Every step, every phase of the program, has to be plotted out. It doesn't make much sense if your training program doesn't match the job.

Before you embark on the training program, you must be sure that you:

- Select a trainee capable of being trained. He or she must have the intelligence, drive, and physical skill the job demands.
- Will be able to use the trained employee—it makes no sense to train someone for nonexistent jobs. The trained employee will be frustrated, and you'll be out your investment.

Successful training is a matter of planning. Before you plunge into your training program, answer these questions compiled by the Small Business Administration.* Think the questions over carefully and answer them honestly.

---

* U.S. Small Business Administration, Management Aids Series, No. 186, 1975.

CHECKLIST FOR DEVELOPING A TRAINING PROGRAM

What Is the Goal of the Training?

The questions in this section are designed to help the owner-manager in defining the objective or goal to be achieved by a training program. Whether the objective is to conduct initial training, to provide for upgrading employees, or to retrain for changing job assignments, the goal should be spelled out before developing the plan for the training program.

		Yes	No
1.	Do you want to improve the performance of your employees?	☐	☐
2.	Will you improve your employees by training them to perform their present tasks better?	☐	☐
3.	Do you need to prepare employees for newly developed or modified jobs?	☐	☐
4.	Is training needed to prepare employees for promotion?	☐	☐
5.	Is the goal to reduce accidents and increase safety practices?	☐	☐
6.	Should the goal be to improve employee attitudes, especially about waste and spoilage practices?	☐	☐
7.	Do you need to improve the handling of materials in order to break production bottlenecks?	☐	☐
8.	Is the goal to orient new employees to their jobs?	☐	☐
9.	Will you need to teach new employees about overall operation?	☐	☐
10.	Do you need to train employees so they can help teach new workers in an expansion program?	☐	☐

What Does the Employee Need to Learn?

Once the objective or goal of the program is set, you will need to determine the subject matter. The following questions are designed to help you decide what the employee needs in terms of duties, responsibilities, and attitudes.

		Yes	No
11.	Can the job be broken down into steps for training purposes?	☐	☐

		Yes	No
12.	Are there standards of quality which trainees can be taught?	☐	☐
13.	Are there certain skills and techniques which trainees must learn?	☐	☐
14.	Are there hazards and safety practices which must be taught?	☐	☐
15.	Have you established the methods which employees must use to avoid or minimize waste and spoilage?	☐	☐
16.	Are there materials-handling techniques that must be taught?	☐	☐
17.	Have you determined the best way for the trainees to operate the equipment?	☐	☐
18.	Are there performance standards which employees must meet?	☐	☐
19.	Are there attitudes that need improvement or modification?	☐	☐
20.	Will information on your products help employees to do a better job?	☐	☐
21.	Should the training include information about the location and use of tool cribs and so on?	☐	☐
22.	Will the employee need instruction about departments other than his own?	☐	☐

What Type of Training?

The type of training to be offered has an important bearing on the balance of the program. Some types lend themselves to achieving all of the objectives or goals, while others are limited. Therefore you should review the advantages of each type in relation to your objective or goal.

		Yes	No
23.	Can you train on-the-job so that employees can produce while they learn?	☐	☐
24.	Should you have classroom training conducted by a paid instructor?	☐	☐
25.	Will a combination of scheduled on-the-job training and vocational classroom instruction work best for you?	☐	☐
26.	Can your goal be achieved with a combination of on-the-job training and correspondence courses?	☐	☐

What Method of Instruction?

One or more methods of instruction may be used. Some are better for one type of training than another: for example, lectures are good for imparting knowledge, and demonstrations are good for teaching skills.

		Yes	No
27.	Does the subject matter call for a lecture or series of lectures?	☐	☐
28.	Should the instructor follow up with discussion sessions?	☐	☐
29.	Does the subject matter lend itself to demonstrations?	☐	☐
30.	Can operating problems be simulated in a classroom?	☐	☐
31.	Can the instructor direct trainees while they perform the job?	☐	☐

What Audiovisual Aids Will You Use?

Audiovisual aids help the instructor to make his points and enable the trainees to grasp and retain the instructions.

		Yes	No
32.	Will a manual of instruction—including job instruction sheets—be used?	☐	☐
33.	Will trainees be given an outline of the training program?	☐	☐
34.	Can outside textbooks and other printed materials be used?	☐	☐
35.	If the training lends itself to the use of motion pictures, film strips, or slides, can you get ones that show the basic operation?	☐	☐
36.	Have you drawings or photographs of the machinery, equipment, or products which could be enlarged and used?	☐	☐
37.	Do you have miniatures or models of machinery and equipment which can be used to demonstrate the operation?	☐	☐

What Physical Facilities Will You Need?

The type of training, the method of instruction, and the audio-visuals will determine the physical facilities needed for the training. In turn, the necessary physical facilities will determine the location of the training. For example, if a certain production machine is necessary, the training would be conducted in the shop.

		Yes	No
38.	If the training cannot be conducted on the production floor, do you have a conference room or a lunchroom in which it can be conducted?	☐	☐
39.	Should the training be conducted off the premises, as in a nearby school, restaurant, hotel or motel?	☐	☐
40.	Will the instructor have the necessary tools, such as a blackboard, lectern, film projector, and a microphone (if needed)?	☐	☐
41.	Will there be sufficient seating and writing surfaces (if needed) for the trainees?	☐	☐
42.	If equipment is to be used, will each trainee be provided with his own?	☐	☐

What About the Timing?

The length of the training program will vary according to the needs of your company, the material to be learned, the ability of the instructor, and the ability of the trainees to learn.

		Yes	No
43.	Should the training be conducted part-time and during working hours?	☐	☐
44.	Should the sessions be held after working hours?	☐	☐
45.	Will the instruction cover a predetermined period of time (for example, 4 weeks, 6 weeks, 3 months)?	☐	☐
46.	Can the length of each session and the number of sessions per week be established?	☐	☐

Who Will Be Selected as Instructor?

The success of training depends to a great extent on the instructor. A qualified one could achieve good results even with limited resources. On the other hand, an untrained instructor may be unsuccessful even with the best program. You may want to use more than one person as instructor.

		Yes	No
47.	Can you fill in as an instructor?	☐	☐
48.	Do you have a personnel manager who has the time and the ability to do the instructing?	☐	☐

	Yes	No
49. Can your foreman or department heads handle the instruction?	☐	☐
50. Should a skilled employee be used as the instructor?	☐	☐
51. Will you have to train the trainer, if he is an employee?	☐	☐
52. Is there a qualified outside instructor available for employment on a part-time basis?	☐	☐

Who Should Be Selected?

Employees should be selected for training on the basis of the goal of the program as well as their aptitudes, physical capabilities, previous experiences, and attitudes.

	Yes	No
53. Should new employees be hired for training?	☐	☐
54. Should the training of new employees be a condition of employment?	☐	☐
55. Would you prefer trainees with previous experience in the work?	☐	☐
56. Are there present employees who need training?	☐	☐
57. Will you consider employees presently in lower-rated jobs who have the aptitude to learn?	☐	☐
58. Is the training to be a condition for promotion?	☐	☐
59. Will the training be made available to handicapped employees whose injury occurred while employed by the company?	☐	☐
60. Will employees be permitted to volunteer for the training?	☐	☐
61. Should employees displaced by job changes, departmental shutdowns, automation, and so on be given the opportunity to be trained in other jobs?		

What Will the Program Cost?

It may be desirable to compute the costs of your training before starting the program. Thus, you can budget sufficient funds for the program and use the budget as a tool for keeping training costs in line.

	Yes	No
62. Should you charge the program for the space, the machines, and materials used?	☐	☐

		Yes	No
63.	Will the wages of trainees be included?	☐	☐
64.	If the instructor is an employee, will his pay be included in the costs?	☐	☐
65.	Will the time you and others spend in preparing and administering the program be part of the costs?	☐	☐
66.	If usable production results from the sessions, should the results of it be deducted from cost of the program?	☐	☐

What Checks or Controls Will You Use?

The results of the training program need to be checked to determine the extent to which the original goal or objective was achieved.

		Yes	No
67.	Can you check the results of the training against the goal or objective?	☐	☐
68.	Can standards of learning time be established against which to check the progress of the trainees?	☐	☐
69.	Can data on trainee performance be developed before, during, and after training?	☐	☐
70.	Will records be kept on the progress of each trainee?	☐	☐
71.	Will trainees be tested on the knowledge and skills acquired?	☐	☐
72.	Will the instructor rate each trainee during, and at the end of, the course?	☐	☐
73.	Will the trainee be followed up periodically by his foreman or department head to determine the long-range effects of his training?	☐	☐
74.	Should you personally check and control the program?	☐	☐

How Should the Program Be Publicized?

Publicizing the company's training program in the community helps attract qualified job applicants. Publicity inside the company helps motivate employees to improve themselves.

		Yes	No
75.	If the program is announced to employees, will the announcement be made before the program starts? During the program?	☐	☐

	Yes	No
76. Are pictures to be taken of the training sessions and used on bulletin boards and in local newspapers?	☐	☐
77. Should employees who complete the training be awarded certificates?	☐	☐
78. Should the certificates be presented at a special affair, such as a dinner?	☐	☐
79. When the certificates are awarded, will you invite the family of the trainees?	☐	☐
80. Should the local newspaper, radio, and TV people be invited to the "graduation" exercises?	☐	☐

Businesses use many different types of training programs. These include:

• On-the-job training. This simply is teaching the trainee the tools of the trade while the trainee is working at his or her job.

• Vestibule training. This involves setting up a joblike situation for the trainee to practice on before attempting the real job.

• Apprenticeship. This is a long process of gradually developing the apprentice into a skilled worker. This form of training is generally used for jobs that demand a variety of complex skills, such as diamond-cutting, carpentry, silversmithing, plumbing, etc.

• Internship. This type of training isn't just reserved for budding doctors. Here, a school and a business form a type of partnership and cooperate to give an individual both schooling and business experience at the same time.

• Outside training. The trainee is sent away from the place of business to learn a skill. Outside training can include college, vocational school, trade school, evening courses, seminars, correspondence school, etc. This method enables the employee to be trained beyond what he or she could learn on the job or in the company.

These are the major types of training programs used today. But for most small businesses one type of training is used overwhelmingly—on-the-job training. Small businesses use this type of program because they can't afford to sit an employee in a vestibule for weeks or months. Small businesses need producers. There are exceptions—plumbers who need an apprentice, small manufacturing plants with highly specialized jobs, and of course, small businessmen who are innovative enough to take advantage of local community college courses. But the meat and potatoes of small business training is on-the-job. Everything else is secondary.

SELECTING THE TRAINER

Who is going to do the training? This is an especially important question with new employees. For the new employee, training is a continuation or even a part of the induction period. It needs to be handled with sensitivity.

Preferably, you the owner will handle the lion's share of the training, because you understand the business best. But there are many occasions when the owner can't be in charge. Then the problem is finding a reliable trainer. Hopefully, you have an excellent employee who can fill the bill. But make sure your trust is well earned.

Marty owned a vacuum franchise which hired salespeople to peddle the vacuums door to door. Marty was under a great deal of financial management pressure, so he left breaking in a new employee to his senior employee, Don, who had been working at the same company for fifteen years. In two days the new employee quit. When asked what happened, all Don said was that the kid couldn't "hack it."

The next week, Marty hired another trainee and placed Don in charge. This employee lasted three days and Don gave the same story. Marty decided that he would check with the trainees who quit and ask them their reasons. It turned out that both told a similar story. They were sorry, but they just couldn't stand the pressures of the job. Both praised Don, said he was very nice and had laid out the responsibilities of the job very clearly. Marty's ex-employees then told him how much business Don had told them they had to bring in each day. Marty was astounded when he heard the figure, which equaled the requirements for an experienced salesman like Don.

Marty saw the light. Don, for some reason, had thrown the new employees to the wolves. He had set the stage for certain failure. Don was a very good salesman, but he was a bad trainer. Further probing by Marty revealed that Don thought today's kids were too soft for selling. He wanted to toughen them up. If they swam, fine. If not, too bad.

Be careful when you select your trainer. There are a bagful of reasons why a good worker wouldn't make a good trainer. Many people aren't patient enough. Envy, competitive feelings, lack of ability to communicate—all could get in the way of training the new employee. The trainer should:

- Be capable of training—must know the job.
- Be willing to train—not feel it's a burden.
- Be understanding and patient enough to teach step by step.
- Be a good example for the trainee to follow.

Even if you do find an excellent trainer, don't eliminate yourself from the training program. Keep a finger in all pies. It's better to anticipate trouble than to have it spring on you unknown.

TRAINING UPPER-LEVEL PERSONNEL

This isn't a real problem for most small businesses. Usually you're the only upper-level employee, and most of the time you hardly consider yourself that. But as your business expands, you may discover a need to hire an assistant manager or someone to perform executive functions.

Training the upper-level employee is different from rank-and-file training. There are no obvious skills to teach, no machines to operate, no shorthand to take. Sure, there are specific elements of a manager's job—the forms to fill out, the way to order materials. But the crux of the upper-level job is management of people and concepts.

You have to be careful in selecting your employees for an executive-type job. Intelligence, drive, ability to lead, ability to make clear decisions are qualities that are necessary. You're going to be trusting this employee with the future of your business.

There are two ways for a small business owner to find a candidate for an executive job—from inside or outside the company. Take a long hard look inside your organization before you hire someone from outside. It's a good source. Look how many mailboys went on to be managers.

But whether you pick from inside or outside the company, the training is basically the same. You take that individual under your wing and you submit him or her to intensive on-the-job training. This has to be your basic approach. Of course you can add trappings, such as sending your employee to business seminars or continuing education courses. But to get a sound manager or executive of any type, you must immerse the trainee into the business he or she will be running in the future. Let them learn by performing all duties. And you'll be right there to help—and also to see if they can succeed at an upper level. If the employee can, you need to know, and if the employee can't hack it, you also need to know—the sooner the better.

EIGHT

Planning Your Own Training Program

Creating the Program / Training Aids / Evaluation /
Retraining Employees for New Jobs

Y OUR TRAINING PROGRAM IS VERY IMPORTANT. TAKE THE
time to do it right.

Almost every small business owner uses the on-the-job training method. Few small businessmen can afford to wait weeks or
months for a new worker to be trained. A productive employee
is needed right away. So, in most cases, training means gradually
increasing the new employee's skills *while he or she is working*.

A major difficulty is rushing the new employee—giving him
or her too much responsibility too fast. For example, if Sam is
assembling telephones, he may be trusted to tighten a few screws
on the first day. Later he can do the whole job, but it must be a
gradual procedure.

The trick to on-the-job training is to provide a good program
and a good instructor. If you just gave Sam a pile of components
and asked him to build a telephone, he'd simply stare at you in
disbelief. But if you sat him down next to your best assembler
and asked Sam to watch, he'd begin to grasp how to do the job.
Still, that wouldn't be enough. Sam has to get his hands into
it—he has to be involved in making phones. So Sam has to have
a teacher—someone who can show him the ropes, someone who
can point out mistakes and praise successes.

CREATING THE PROGRAM

Before you can create a training program, you must go back to square one. Check your job analysis. There are two things you must know:

- What skills does the employee lack?
- What skills does the job require?

Your objective is to match employee skills with job needs.

It always helps to put it all down on paper. Each new employee isn't a special case. Your training program must be standardized for the target job so you can turn out trained employees with the same skills. This doesn't mean that the target job can never be changed. If your business grows—or diminishes—to the extent that a job's duties change, then the training program must be changed to meet new needs. But as long as the job remains the same, the program must be standardized to give results which are as identical as possible.

In most small businesses you, the owner, are the one who guides a new employee through training. Many owners believe that the best approach is to provide a few preliminary instructions and then turn the employee loose on the job until he or she hits a problem. It's very tempting to train people this way. After all, the owner has a business to run and often "can't be bothered" by trainee problems. But the end result of this management style is that the trainee will run to you with every little problem if you're sympathetic. If you're gruff or impatient, the trainee will avoid you, even when legitimate problems arise.

In any event, allowing a trainee to run loose is unproductive. Even if you can't provide full guidance, you can set up a graduated program which will train systematically. First, acquaint the trainee with all of the job's duties. Then set up a schedule to follow. For example, Sam, the phone assembler, might learn how to assemble the housing during the first week and then advance to internal assembly during the second and third weeks. While the trainee is learning the job, you must be in a position to evaluate the work. Is the schedule too slow or too fast? Is the work progressing satisfactorily? Don't be misled by believing that once you get the trainee started, your job is done. No matter how busy you are, get personally involved with the trainee's work. Talk to him or her. See if there are any problems. Ask for comments or suggestions about the training program. Get to know the person and the work.

TRAINING AIDS

On-the-job training can be bolstered by any other form of training described in the last chapter. There are no impassable boundaries between the different types of training styles. For example, you may want to use written guides. Written instructions which carefully describe each step of a task are used in most restaurants. They are called breakdown sheets. A chef's breakdown sheet may tell how to roast a turkey. A bartender's breakdown sheet would tell him or her how to concoct a Singapore Sling. A waiter's breakdown sheet may show how to arrange the salad bar.

Written instructions can be used for almost any type of job: stock clerks learning which shelf is which; sales personnel learning how their products are used; factory workers learning how to operate equipment. But don't rely only on a written guide. At best, it's a supplement to supervision. It's there to remind the trainee how to perform this or that step.

The same applies to lectures, audiovisual aids, or outside schooling. If they appear to be helpful, they should be considered. Your goal is to elevate the trainee's skills up to the level the job requires, as soon as possible—and with as little cost as possible to your business. Anything which helps you reach your goal is desirable.

To summarize, your training program should:

- Be carefully planned, using the job analysis as guide.
- Provide a schedule for the trainee to follow.
- Allow for your personal evaluation of the trainee's progress.
- Allow for your evaluation of the program itself.
- Use any training aid which may help, including written instructions.

EVALUATION

A final, and very necessary, part of the training program is its overall evaluation. You have to know whether or not it was a success.

The two questions you have to ask are:

- Did the trainee learn all that was necessary?
- Was the training program as efficient as possible?

The first question is relatively easy to answer. How well is the trainee producing? Is he or she struggling? Making many mistakes? Are you constantly correcting his or her work? If so, is the fault with the person or the program? By the time the trainee has become immersed in the program, you should have a good idea of his or her potential. If the trainee completes the program with flying colors and then falls down on the job, the program is probably faulty.

Answering the second question is much more difficult. You can't afford the big-name consultants who come into giant corporations and create training organizations for hundreds of thousands of dollars. Since your training program is essentially informal, you have to rely on your own instincts. Keep asking yourself: "Is there a better way to present this concept or teach that step?" Don't let yourself become complacent about training. Keep it vital, instructive, and interesting. And always keep in touch with the trainee. Monitor progress throughout the program. Know how the new employee is handling different facets of the new job. If you keep informed at all times, you'll know how your training program is functioning—and you won't run into any unpleasant surprises.

RETRAINING EMPLOYEES FOR NEW JOBS

Retraining in a small organization is somewhat easier than starting from scratch with someone new. You know all there is to know about the individual you've selected to be trained—both capabilities and deficiencies. All the same, you have to apply the same criteria while training the old employee. Once in the program, he or she is just another trainee. At times, the old employee will present special problems, maybe a know-it-all attitude that can be very destructive to progress. You have to be firm and decisive in these cases. Whether new or old, the trainee has to be taught all the necessary skills. Your future productivity depends on it.

Part III

PEOPLE MANAGEMENT

Communications

COMMUNICATION IS A NEWFANGLED WORD FOR AN OLD-fashioned idea—it is a term overused and much abused. A complicated business has grown up around the word in the last fifty years. *Communication* simply means trying to understand people and making an effort to get through to them. The shortest route possible is the best one—straight and direct.

Communication between you and your employees is the most important aspect of people management. Good communication keeps you and your employees in touch with each other—it creates a bond.

First, exactly what is involved in communication? It is the free flow of concepts, instructions, and ideas between employer and employees. In large organizations, communications are complex. There are various managerial levels through which information flows. To do the job properly, big businesses create their own internal communications departments. They publish house organs (magazines or newspapers), produce training films and slide shows, and send employees to school—all to get the company's message to the employees.

A small business isn't as complex, but the basic communication problems remain the same. In fact, communication can be difficult in a business with only two people—as many husband-wife teams have discovered. There always will be difficulties when one person attempts to convey something to another person, because human beings are different. You, the owner, may think certain instructions are perfectly clear, yet your employee may be left totally in the dark. If nothing is done to remedy the situation—for example, if the employee is afraid to ask for clarification—your instructions, and maybe an entire job, will be botched.

DEVELOPING MUTUAL UNDERSTANDING

Business communications involve more than just telling your employees what to do. For communication to be ideal, there has to be mutual understanding. The employee must understand what you say, and you need to understand the employee's position, level of understanding, and attitude. Communication doesn't work any other way.

John was an old-style manager who believed in telling his gas station employees what to do. He never asked their opinions or stopped to discover if they understood instructions. He just barked out gruff orders, creating intense job dissatisfaction. John was also old-fashioned in his approach to his business. He kept as far away from foreign cars as possible, regardless of the fact that two of his mechanics were experienced with foreign makes and felt business could be improved if they were allowed to work on the imports. They tried telling John, but he refused to consider their ideas. He ordered them never to bring up the subject again.

John made many obvious mistakes based on bad communications. He refused to sit down and consider his employee's ideas—ideas which happened to be excellent. In addition, he was abusive when they tried to open up channels themselves. The end result was that his two mechanics quit and opened a competing business. Bull-headed to the end, John kept managing his business in the same fashion until there was no business left to manage.

With John, communications went only in one direction. When he spoke, he expected employees to jump. His reasoning was that the gas station was his business, and his alone. He had a feudal lord's concept of power. Employees were paid to do as told—it was as simple as that. The only communications were his instructions. And you'll see in the next chapter, on motivation, that's not the way to treat employees.

Most of the time, an owner's mistakes won't be so obvious. In fact, the owner may feel that communications are fine and all is well. But is it really? Do you take time to actually listen to what the employee is saying?

When Oscar listened to one of his clerks, he would sit back in his thick leather chair, gaze steadily at the clerk, and think about where he would go for lunch while the employee was spilling out his heart. Oscar knew how to interpret tones, and he would give a noncommittal grunt or a slight nod when the conversation demanded a response. But he never really analyzed what the clerk was trying to get across. All he did was give the appearance of listening. The poor clerk went away happy at first. But when none of his suggestions were acted upon, frustration grew.

So remember that a very important part of communications is listening, actually involving yourself in your employee's point of view—and not only for the employee's benefit. Not by a long shot. Feedback—getting employee response—is invaluable in any business. Your employees are the ones who are implementing your plans and instructions. If they are dissatisfied with the instructions, don't understand your plans, or may have an idea about how to upgrade part of the plan—you want to hear from them.

Art was a driver for a delivery business. He had received instructions to alter his route to include new business. At the same time, he was given a list of territories other drivers would be servicing. Art was a bright, conscientious worker. He saw a way to combine two overlapping territories so that mileage would be cut by a third. Luckily, Art's boss, Ted, was receptive to employee ideas. Art had no problem seeing Ted and communicating his plan. The plan saved the company hundreds of dollars in gas and depreciation during the year. Ted was happy to save the money and was pleased that his employees were able to contribute to the business. Art was pleased that his plan was accepted. He felt a part of the business. Ted had listened to him, had seen the value of his idea. Art knew he belonged, was a working part of the company, and he was satisfied.

It's also important to listen and evaluate ideas that won't work. Sandy came to Ted with an idea about how to expand business to a nearby state. Ted listened carefully, then explained why the idea wouldn't work because of differing state regulations. Ted made sure he told Sandy the idea was terrific—that the regulations made it impossible. Again, Ted was pleased that his employees were thinking about the business. Sandy was satisfied. He didn't go away feeling demeaned or unfairly turned away. He knew he had been given a fair hearing and was a valuable, working part of the delivery business.

Similarly, if your employees just can't fathom your instructions, you need the line of communication open so that you can clear up any problem. After all, it helps to have a worker understand what's going on before he or she attempts a task. If your employees fear you, feel you are unsympathetic or uninterested, they will try to guess what's in your mind. Far better to make your employees feel comfortable enough to talk out any problems they have with you. Time, money, employee satisfaction, and peace of mind are the rewards of good communications.

KNOW YOUR EMPLOYEES

Hopefully, in a small business, you get to know your employees and know them well. You understand individual idiosyncrasies and different temperaments. All this is important in maintaining communications, too. Remember, we're all different. One employee may interpret your instructions one way and another in a completely different fashion.

George, owner of a florist shop, understood his three employees. He knew that Bill was the most conscientious and could always be relied on to clean his working area without being told. Harold was different. George not only had to give more specific instructions to Harold, but also needed to tell him what time the task should be finished. George knew that Harold could do good work but that he had to be pushed. The third employee, Dorothy, presented yet a different problem. Like Harold, she couldn't be left on her own, but since she created floral arrangements she considered herself to be more of an artist and expected special treatment. This was fine as far as George was concerned. She did an excellent job. When George gave instructions to Dorothy he carefully phrased the orders as suggestions—"Would you mind working on the fern arrangements now, please?"

George had a close working relationship with all his employees. He knew that Bill could be dealt with in a straightforward manner; Harold had to be given detailed orders; and Dorothy needed to be treated with kid gloves. George handled all three by good communication and good management.

Every employee should be treated with respect, but there are some cases, like Harold's, where it is best to give instructions clearly, precisely, and authoritatively. This is where good communication comes in. George had to have a two-way flow of information and a good understanding of his employees, or he never would have made the distinctions between different personalities. He knew that if he tried to order Bill to perform tasks the same way he ordered Harold, there would be big trouble. Bill would resent him and quit.

Knowing your employees is a big part of communication. In a small business, you're lucky to be in a position where it is easy to get to know your workers.

ATTITUDES

It's not enough to understand employee attitudes. You have to be aware of your own attitude as well. How do you approach a new idea? Like this? "Say, Sam, I'd like you to try something new today. It probably won't work very well—I'm sure there are too many bugs in it. But try and give it your best shot, okay?" How do you think Sam is going to feel about the new plan? You've programmed defeat into it before it's been given a chance. If you want something to work, keep a positive attitude: "Hey, Sam, I've come up with a great plan that should make the job easier and increase productivity by twenty percent. I really think it's going to be big. And I'd like you to get started on it right away." Quite a difference. Of course, you should give your employee all the facts. If there are some rough edges, show where they are, but never say die.

Attitude can be transmitted in many different ways. Words alone may mean less than the way they are said. Think of the many ways a simple "uh-huh" can be expressed. An employee walks into your office and asks you for an undeserved raise. You look him straight in the eye, your facial muscles tense, your arms crossed in front of you. You stand up, maintaining eye contact all the time, and just say "Uh-huh" in a short, clipped tone. What do you think that conveys to the employee? No way is he going to get a raise.

You unconsciously can offend or demoralize with your nonverbal attitude. An employee rushes into your office and says he needs your advice quickly. But you're busy with something else. So without really hearing him out, you say "Uh-huh, sure, sure," while you shuffle through some papers. The employee feels slighted or uncomfortable, even though you meant no harm.

Communication means mutual understanding, and understanding yourself. Read the feedback. How well do you work with your employees? Do they feel comfortable in your presence, or are you someone to be avoided? Do they respect your opinions, or do they ignore your instructions? Don't expect to always win the "most loved boss" award. There will be conflicts—and you are the boss. But if you are fair with your employees and make every effort to understand them, your business will generally run smoothly, and you'll be communicating.

INFORMING YOUR EMPLOYEES

Exactly how do you keep in touch with your employees? Your employees have to be made aware of business facts. Larger companies publish magazines for employees. In a small business like yours, you seldom even need to write a memo. It's good for business to let your employees know the successes and failures. They get the "big picture" and feel closer to the business. If you can't remember to keep your employees informed by word of mouth, then write them a few notes, maybe at the end of the week—or when something important happens. Then invite them to discuss the memos with you. If you were successful at something, analyze why. And if there was a failure, pinpoint the reason. But involve and inform your employees. Not only does it keep the lines of communication open, but it motivates the workers.

This works in reverse, too. Encourge your employees to write out any suggestions they may have. There should be a system in your business for employees to air problems or offer ideas. The old standby, the suggestion box, is one tried way. But for this to be successful, you have to read what is given to you. And then let the employee know that you did read what he or she suggested. Nothing is more worthless than a stack of unread suggestions or a group of employees who feel they won't be heard.

Communications encompasses many things. As the owner of a business, you know that giving instructions is a major portion of the communications. It's surprising how many managers can't give good instructions. Henry drove his employees wild. Whenever he thought of something, he would go and tell them. He was in and out of his office all day, adding on to instructions, modifying them. The result was pure confusion.

Know exactly what the instructions are that you want to give. Work them out for yourself, and in detail. Think about the instructions before you give them. Did you forget anything? The time to modify orders is before they are given, not while they are being carried out.

Also, before you hand out instructions, make sure that they are clear. Will your employees understand them? If you have to give long, involved orders, break them down into smaller, easily understood parts.

The next step is actually giving the instructions to the employee. Take your time. Don't rush through them. Speak clearly and make sure that you are understood. Ask questions. See if your employee understood the instructions. Be patient. Answer all questions. Then make sure that the questioner understood the response. You've seen many people who shake their heads knowingly, even though they don't understand one word. Some people try to grasp a concept and even ask a question, but few are willing to ask a second or third question about the same problem.

That brings us to the last step, the follow-up. Get involved in the instructions yourself. See if anyone is having problems on the job. Sometimes it's hard to translate concepts into actual work. It's up to you to smooth out the problems and, again, answer any new questions.

A GOOD COMMUNICATIONS NETWORK

Communications are the bones of the business, what holds it up. The better the communications in a business, the smoother it will run. But it's not easy to instill a good communications network in any business, large or small. It takes hard work. You have to know your employees. You have to know how to talk to them, and just as important, you have to know how to listen to them.

The important steps are:

- Free flow of concepts and information.
- Mutual understanding.
- Careful listening.
- Knowing your employee, understanding him or her.
- Open channels.
- Good attitude.
- Receiving suggestions—reading and working on them.
- Clear presentation of instructions.

Communication is a tool. Use it to touch your employees, to involve them in the business. It is one of the strongest motivaters there is.

TEN

Motivating Your People

It Takes More Than Money / Elements of Motivation

"**H**OW DO I GET THEM TO GET OFF THEIR CANS AND DO what I tell 'em?" The age-old question. It's driven many managers and owners up the wall and beyond the bend. But many managers are stymied because they often look at their productivity in terms of statistics—numbers on a computer printout.

As the owner of a small business, you may make the mistake of treating your employees just like your machinery. Push a button here, try a little oil there—if nothing works, get a replacement.

Your employees aren't machines. They bear absolutely no resemblance to a drill-press or a typewriter. The new employee doesn't come complete with a service manual and a number to call in case of breakdown.

The first thing to understand when dealing with people is that there is no cut-and-dried approach. Everyone has the same basic needs—for example, to be paid—but every employee has a special personality.

In the last chapter you saw how important communication is. And understanding your employees is a major part of communication. To motivate your employees, you also need to understand them.

IT TAKES MORE THAN MONEY

In the old days, the owner of a business was a dictator. He or she sat behind a big desk and commanded workers with an iron will. And they obeyed, because he or she held all the strings. Any sign of trouble, and the employee would be kicked out. This meant no money and no way to support a family. Survival was the objective.

As workers began to get more rights, earn more money, and become more than chattels, attitudes began to change. Money wasn't enough. Workers began to demand more benefits, better facilities, more security. And it wasn't just the workers—scientists began to discover that certain intangible items, such as job satisfaction, motivated the employee more efficiently than higher pay.

Today, an employee needs more than a fat paycheck to keep him or her happy.

Jim repaired typewriters for a small company that sold used typewriters and serviced broken ones. He had worked for the company for three years. His work was beyond reproach. Suddenly, his supervisor discovered many mistakes. Customers were returning typewriters Jim had fixed. This went on for several weeks, the complaints mounting. The owner of the business at last decided to talk to him. Jim's first excuse was that he was angry because he felt he wasn't getting enough money. The owner kept pressing him—was that all? Jim had a complaint about working conditions. It turned out that the start of the problem had been when Jim's work area had been switched away from a window in the shop and stuck off in a corner. Jim felt that he had been slighted by the move. The solution was simple. Jim was returned to his window. His work improved rapidly, and everyone was happy again.

The point is that many times grievances are expressed in terms of "more money"—no matter what the real problem. The owner may increase an employee's salary, only to discover renewed demands and no improvement. Don't make the opposite mistake in thinking that money doesn't matter—it sure does. Every employee deserves and needs a fair wage or salary. But it shouldn't stop there. No owner should say, "I pay you well, so you should do everything I tell you to do."

What motivates a person? Management books are chock-full of graphs, formulas, and theories. What it all boils down to is that every employee needs more than a nine-to-five, earn-the-money existence. When your employee leaves home at eight in the morning, he or she doesn't turn into a completely different person. Sure, an employee has a home life and a job life. But they're both a part of the employee's life; the two "lives" aren't separable. The employee has the same desires, ambitions, intelligence, and sense of humor at work as at home. The personality that operates the drill-press is the same one that drinks a beer after work. In short, the employee needs a meaningful job.

Joe worked for a stereo repair shop. He was one of three employees. Joe was an excellent repairman, but it wasn't enough. He wanted to design stereo systems and install them—to create his own sound systems. But there was little communication between him and his boss. His boss wanted Joe to work on an assembly line with the other two employees. Joe was to repair speakers while the other two men worked on different components. Joe's love for his job vanished. He needed the money—which was good—so he kept on working. But to him work was a time of sacrifice. He exchanged this amount of his time for this many dollars. There was no enjoyment, no personal involvement, no challenge—just fix those speakers and get out. Joe lived for weekends and vacations.

Of course, this is how plenty of people view their jobs. A sacrifice to be made in order to get money. But these are the people who take no pride in their work—forget a screw here, a bolt there. The choice is yours—do you want your employee to feel a part of the business, or like a stranger who takes the money and runs?

ELEMENTS OF MOTIVATION

An interested employee generally is the best employee. Someone who gets involved with the work, thinks about the job, and enjoys it. You can help create this type of employee by making sure almost any job has satisfying elements.

Behavioral scientists call it job enrichment. Basically, it means getting the employee out of the same old rut—the day-in, day-out, nonstop, never-changing task. Variety is the spice of life, so the idea is to put a little variety into a job. A stock clerk may help handle sales occasionally, an assembler may work on different parts of the product instead of just one, a repairman may be rotated with another repairman.

Actually, there is more opportunity for job enrichment in a small business than a large one. The small business owner can't afford to hire specialists. If you rely on two or three employees, usually those employees have to be jacks-of-all-trades. If you own a small gourmet food shop, your original plan may be to hire someone to stack the shelves, arrange the delivery area, sweep up, dust the shelves, and stamp the prices on the merchandise. But after a while this employee will also be handling the cash register, ordering new supplies, and maybe even thinking about new merchandise that would sell well.

This is the type of employee you want. Someone who can take satisfaction in the job and become a part of the business. The last thing you want is an employee who doesn't feel a part of the business, who feels like a stranger or interloper on your turf. Because once the employee identifies with a business, he or she is motivated to make that business succeed.

Job satisfaction and a sense of belonging to the business are important motivators. They help create a sense of achievement, of self-esteem, and of job security. Add sufficient money to the mix, and you have created many of the conditions that you need in order to develop and hold a strong and stable work force.

Your role as owner/manager is to attempt to help the employee with these motivators. For an employee to feel self-esteem, praise him or her in front of others, offer a compatible salary. Be liberal with recognition. Everybody needs it. Why do so many people pull crazy stunts to get into the Guinness Book of World Records? Why do entertainers bask in applause? Recognition by fellow human beings. Many businesses recognize this need and offer awards, banquets honoring employees, and recognition bonuses. No reason you can't do the same thing in a smaller way. In addition to any gain, rewards are a terrific way of boosting an employee's ego—and making him or her identify with the business even more strongly.

Of course, basic human needs must be met. Physical safety, a reasonable place to work, reasonable hours, a fair salary and benefits. But once these have been met, you have to work on the employee's more personal needs. Everyone wants to be respected, belong to something, and feel good about his or her work.

Still, you can't expect your business to be a Garden of Eden. There always will be differences of opinions, crises, and an occasional bad apple. As you'll see in the next chapter, on supervision, you have to remain fair and be consistent. If you truly believe that it is important that your employees feel a concern about your business—as if it were their business—you'll listen to grievances and hear out problems they perceive. Good communication is vital if employee and owner are to know each other's minds.

What you can't do is reward favorites and withhold rewards from other employees you don't like so well. For example, Fred owned a small newspaper. He had six people working in an editorial capacity. His newest employee was Tom, the son of a close friend. The young man had been working on the paper for less than a year, but Fred really took a shine to him. Within the year, Tom had been promoted over the heads of all but the oldest employee—and he was worried. Tom was competent—but he wasn't another Ernest Hemingway. The point is that the young man was fed a great many motivators—recognition, salary increases, job satisfaction—but at the cost of total dissatisfaction on the part of the other employees. Suddenly the others lost their feelings of security and self-esteem. The owner had suddenly become alien, with reasonable promotion policies thrown to the four winds.

In this case, Fred was not justified in his actions. They weren't taken to help the business. They were taken because he wanted to move his friend's son up the ladder. In some businesses there are excellent reasons to promote talent over the heads of deadwood. And in some cases, promotions like that motivate the deadwood to work a little harder. But in Fred's case it was owner prejudice. And predictably, three of his employees quit suddenly and left him in the lurch.

Motivation is a complex subject. To make it work, you should get to know each of your employees—know what makes them tick. Money isn't everything in a job. When money isn't an issue, there will always be other issues. But if you remember that your employees also consider your business "theirs," and have certain rights in the business, you'll have come a long way toward recognizing what the important motivators are.

ELEVEN

Supervision

Don't Try to Do It All Yourself / Delegation /
Your Role as Supervisor / Two Dozen Ideas
for Effective Administration

S UPERVISION COVERS QUITE A LOT OF GROUND IN A SMALL
business. You, the owner, are both top and middle management. There are no intermediaries in your business. You are
everything. The combination is often difficult to reconcile.

What is the supervisor's job? Basically, a supervisor manages
people. He or she directs others in the execution of their work.
The supervisor is responsible for the smooth accomplishment of
all tasks.

The supervisor's main product is the productivity of his or her
employees. In a large business, a supervisor receives orders as
well as giving them. In a small business, the owner initiates the
orders and also gives them directly.

As owner, you see the "big picture" at all times. You have
more than people management on your mind. There are production schedules, ordering, storing, financial statements—many
things you must take care of and coordinate, along with the
work of your employees. That juggling is what business is all
about. You can't neglect one for another, you must always
strike a balance.

Your job as supervisor is a complex one. Good communication and the ability to motivate are your best tools. Again, as
supervisor, step one is to understand your employees. Remem-

ber, your job is to get them to do what you want them to do—their jobs. There are three elements of a supervisor's job:

- If something is wrong, analyze the problem and correct it.
- If everything is running smoothly, know why and maintain it.
- If everything is running smoothly, try to figure out how you can make it run even better.

Fix, maintain, and improve the productivity of your business. In this, your employees are the key.

DON'T TRY TO DO IT ALL YOURSELF

Many people still have a very old-fashioned view of supervisors. To them, supervisors are supposed to butt into everything, watch every move a subordinate makes, and constantly crack the whip. On the contrary, it is essential that the supervisor *not* butt into everything—employees work best when they are given room to maneuver and grow. Everyone needs some independence.

Small business owners sometimes think they have to know everything and control everything. Employees become automatons. A small business owner with this attitude will have serious problems.

Richard was the owner of a bicycle shop. As the bike boom grew, he grew. He grew to ten employees. Business was terrific, but Richard just couldn't relax. He felt that he had to do everything, since he was in charge. His employees grew used to his stamp on everything. They didn't make a move without his approval.

Suddenly Richard became seriously ill and had to be hospitalized for several months. His employees, leaderless and with no confidence in themselves, floundered from crisis to crisis. Since Richard had insisted on personally dealing with the manufacturers, his employees had difficulty taking over. The new man who succeeded Richard did badly in dealing with employees. The mechanics, sensing the change, slacked off. Absenteeism and lateness grew. By the time Richard returned, his bicycle store was on the skids.

Richard was good, too good. Successful businesspeople need to be excellent—that's what made their businesses succeed. And quite correctly, many times they feel that they could do any job better than their employees. That's where the trouble starts. Even if the owner is the best at everything, he or she can't do everything. If the employee is forced to do only the time-consuming dirty work—filling out forms, turning bolts, cleaning up—while the owner flits from one station to another like the good fairy, making a decision here and giving an order there, the employee is turned into a non-thinking machine, dependent on the boss for all ideas and inspiration. As business grows, more and more people run to you with all sorts of problems, trivial and serious. Then you sit back and wonder why your working days always seem to be twelve hours long, filled with trivia.

Even if the boss enjoys a twelve-hour trivia-filled day, it's unhealthy for any company to be controlled by one indispensable person. A major motivator for employees is personally involving themselves in the business. If the owner makes all the decisions, that limits or completely cuts out the involvement of others.

DELEGATION

You don't want to work twelve-hour days and you do want to involve your employees. What's the answer? Delegation. It's very simple. You have to cut the umbilical cord and let your employees start thinking and doing on their own. First, delegation isn't surrendering all responsibility—it's still your company. You must delegate authority wisely to employees who can handle it. You're putting someone in charge of an important part of your business. You want that person to be well prepared and qualified. You don't want to capriciously turn over the reins to just anyone.

The employees to whom you delegate responsibility must be capable of working on their own, initiating new ideas and carrying them out. It is also very important that they know the limits of their authority.

Karl had been given charge of a production line. Soon he began to monopolize the delivery department. He got his materials first and fastest. But it wasn't enough. When material ran short, he began to order replacements on his own. This threw the entire ordering and delivering system of the business out of whack. Soon other supervisors began complaining, and the business was thrown into an uproar. Karl was an excellent supervisor, and got fantastic results—but at the expense of others. The owner had to explain to Karl the exact limits of his authority plus the importance of working through the proper channels, and then had to periodically check Karl's operations for a while.

As your business grows, learn to turn loose. A major question you need constantly to answer is how would the business function if you weren't there? Sit down and ask yourself: "If I were sick in bed for a month, what would happen to my business?" It's a sobering question—a question not many owners care to linger over. If your answer is "It would fall apart in twenty minutes," then you need a better organization. Your business won't run in your head. If you expand, or diversify, you must bring others in. It's good for your business and good for your employees' morale and sense of worth.

Keep your hands on the reins, but learn where to loosen up. Let your employees have some rope, but not enough to hang you. While you should allow them to carry out individual actions, always check for results. If an employee is failing, it's time to yank on the reins. The business is the primary consideration. You have to allow freedom which produces positive results. Never feel reluctant to discuss shortcomings. People should be given a chance, even a couple of chances, and worked with to improve results, but if they just can't cut it, step up to the problem and remove them. This is part and parcel of your role as supervisor. It's the exact spot where many supervisors falter.

YOUR ROLE AS SUPERVISOR

Just because you delegate some of your authority, don't forget where you stand in your business. There are certain intangibles a good supervisor provides. One is a sense of direction. You have to set an example by being positive about the work, enthusiastic about new challenges. Embrace everything new with optimism.

As owner/supervisor, you also set the goals for your employees to follow. Setting goals includes good communications and motivation. Your employees must know what you're shooting for. It's better to inform your employees that you want (and the business needs) two thousand whatzits by the end of the week, than to tell them to increase production without giving a reason. The two thousand whatzits are a goal to shoot for, an objective to reach.

What it all boils down to is that you are the leader. Ultimately, you direct where the business is going. And the final responsibility is always yours. You hand out assignments, but you also set examples of how to follow the guidelines.

This is why the supervisor's role is difficult. A supervisor has to worry about his or her own actions at all times. If a supervisor considers an employee a loser, the circle completes itself when the employee begins to believe it. It's the power of the position. So why not turn attitudes around? Approach employees with a positive attitude and tell them there's nothing they can't do—they can rise to all occasions.

The owner/supervisor should:

- Lead.
- Provide an example.
- Be understanding.
- Motivate.
- Delegate.

Don't:

- Try to do everything.
- Oversupervise.
- Be inconsistent.
- Be negative.

The SBA has a useful synopsis of effective administration ideas.*

---

* U.S. Small Business Administration, Management Aids Series, No. 19, 1971.

TWO DOZEN IDEAS FOR EFFECTIVE ADMINISTRATION

The ideas which follow are aimed primarily at top managers of small business. They are by no means all the thoughts on a very complex subject, but they do seem helpful in answering two rather fundamental questions:

- What is the main job of the chief operating executive in a small manufacturing concern?
- What are the administrative goals which he should strive to attain?

Individual opinions on the role of the top administrator vary. "To organize, visualize, energize, supervise," says Lounsbury S. Fish, organization counsel for the Standard Oil Company of California. "To maintain a system of cooperative effort," says Chester I. Barnard, president of the Rockefeller Foundation. "To achieve a balanced relationship between the logical organization of operations and the social organization of teamwork," says Fritz J. Roethlisberger, professor of human relations at the Harvard Business School.

What these definitions boil down to is perhaps basically this: The job of the administrator is to get things done through people and to make his concern a good place in which to work.

Here are two dozen practical ideas on successful administration gathered from the experience of many successful business leaders. The ideas are worth a good deal of careful thought, for they can help you to do your job better in building an alert, effective, responsible staff.

1. *Emphasize skill, not rules, in your organization.* Judge your own actions and those of your subordinates by their effects—effects in terms of increasing both the competitive strength of your business and the satisfaction of the human needs of the people who work in it. Go easy on pat rules for running a business. Doing it "by the book" isn't always the most satisfactory way. If an unorthodox solution works effectively and pleases the people who use it, don't discount it just because it doesn't seem exactly "according to Hoyle."

2. *Set a high standard for your organization.* If you are irregular in your work habits, late for appointments, fuzzy in expressing yourself, careless about facts, bored in attitude, your executives probably will be, too. If, on the other hand, you set a high standard for the organization, in all probability your executives will be eager to follow your good example.

3. *Know your subordinates and try to determine what is important to each.* Continuous study of individuals is a "must" for getting things done through people. Motives and attitudes are important tools for the executive, and they can be determined only by study. Since security is

the main drive in many people, giving recognition to the contribution of others and to their role in your concern is a useful starting point in getting the best from men of future executive caliber.

Individuals vary widely in their other characteristics. Well-timed praise may spur one person to new heights of achievement, but it may only inflate another. A better key to the latter's effort might be constructive criticism. A third individual may wilt under any kind of criticism, and some other approach is needed. The skillful executive constantly hunts for the appropriate procedure. He also searches beyond the office for background. People's motives and attitudes are heavily conditioned by their personal situations. For this reason, tactful drawing-out of subordinates can often supply invaluable information for understanding them. Remember that people often act on the basis of emotional, nonlogical reasons, even though they try to appear completely logical.

4. *Try to listen thoughtfully and objectively.* The executive who knows his people—their habits, worries, ambitions, touchy points, and pet prides—comes to appreciate why they behave as they do and what motives stir them. The best and fastest way to know them is to encourage them to talk freely, without fear of ridicule or disapproval. Try to understand how others actually feel on a subject, whether or not you feel the same way. Never dominate a conversation or meeting by doing all the talking yourself if you want to find out where your people stand. If both you and one of your people start to say something at the same time, give him the right of way.

One objection to the idea of being a good listener is that it takes time to draw people out. The answer is that it takes time to plan, too. Both are essential in the executive's job. The time invested will pay big dividends.

5. *Be considerate.* Few things contribute more to building a hard-working executive team than a considerate chief. Try to be calm and courteous toward your lieutenants. Consider the effects on them of any decisions you make. Take into account the problems they have of their own, both business and personal. Try to build up their pride in their work, and their self-respect. Start by treating personal characteristics as assets and being careful not to trample on them.

6. *Be consistent.* If you "fly off the handle" and "set off fireworks," you are likely to frighten subordinates into their shells; if you vacillate wildly in reaction, mood, and manner, you will probably bewilder them. Neither sort of behavior can win you the confidence and cooperation of your lieutenants, which you must have to get things done.

You and your junior executives are in the position of a leader and his followers. One wants to follow only the leader whose course is steady and whose actions are predictable.

7. *Give your subordinates objectives and a sense of direction.* Subordinates should know where they're going, what they're doing, and why they're doing it, in order to plan their time intelligently and to work effectively. Good junior executives seldom enjoy working just day to day. Therefore, make clear the relation between their day-to-day work and the larger company objectives.

For example, don't merely ask people to analyze the variable costs of a particular department. Tell them also that it's part of a longer-range plan to provide leeway for salary increases, and that the knowledge they provide will strengthen the operating efficiency of your company.

8. *Give your directions in terms of suggestions or requests.* If your people have initiative and ability, you will get vastly better results in this way than you will by giving orders or commands. Issue the latter only as a last resort. If you find that you *have* to give orders all the time, maybe you'd better look for some new assistants—or re-examine the way you have been handling your own job. Be sure, also, to tell why you want certain things done. Informal, oral explanations are often as good or better than written ones; let the individual circumstances be your guide here.

9. *Delegate responsibility for details to subordinates.* This is another "obvious" point that is frequently overlooked. Delegating responsibility is basic to competent administration. You are not doing your real job as an executive if you do not delegate, because, as the chief executive, if you insist on keeping your hand in details, you discourage your subordinates by competing with them. Moreover, by doing everything yourself, you prevent subordinates from learning to make their own decisions. Sooner or later the capable ones will quit and the others will sit back and let you do all the work. Ultimately, you will have no time for the thinking and the planning that are the most important parts of your job. Think of your executives as working *with* you, not *for* you.

10. *Show your staff that you have faith in them and that you expect them to do their best.* Junior executives—and everyone else, for that matter—tend to perform according to what is expected of them. If they know you have the confidence in them to expect a first-rate job, that's what they will usually try to give you.

11. *Keep your subordinates informed.* Bring them up to date constantly on new developments, and let them know well in advance whenever changes are in the offing. As members of a team, they are entitled

to know what's going on. If they do, their thinking will be geared more closely to reality and their attitudes will be more flexible. Give them enough information about conditions and events in your company and industry to let them see themselves and their work in perspective.

12. *Let your assistants in on your plans at an early stage.* It's true that many plans can't be discussed very far in advance. They should, however, be discussed with subordinates before they are in final form. It will give your assistants that all-important chance to participate. Furthermore, because they will have taken part in shaping the plan, it will be as much theirs as yours, and they will feel a personal responsibility for its success. Hence, they will usually carry out the program with vigor and precision.

13. *Ask subordinates for their counsel and help.* Bring them actively into the picture. It will help to give them a feeling of "belonging" and to build their self-confidence. It will often make them eager to work harder than ever. What is just as important, they may well have good ideas which may never be utilized unless you ask for them.

14. *Give a courteous hearing to ideas from subordinates.* Many ideas may sound fantastic to you, but it's important not to act scornful or impatient. There's no surer way to discourage original thinking by a subordinate than to disparage or ridicule a suggestion he makes. His next idea might well be the very one you want—make it easy for that next idea to come to you.

15. *Give your subordinates a chance to take part in decisions.* When your people feel they have had a say in a decision, they are much more likely to go along with it cooperatively. If they agree with the decision, they will look at it as their own and back it to the hilt. If they don't agree, they may still back it more strongly than otherwise because of the fact that their point of view was given full and fair consideration.

16. *Tell the originator of an idea what action was taken and why.* If you do so, he'll study other problems and make suggestions on ways to solve them. If his idea is accepted, he will be encouraged by seeing the results of his thinking put into effect. If his idea is not adopted, he will accept that fact more readily and with fuller understanding if you show him that the reasons for rejection are clear and sound. In addition, knowing exactly why his idea was impractical will help the suggester analyze the next problem more clearly.

17. *Try to let people carry out their own ideas.* It occasionally happens that equally good suggestions on a particular problem come from two individuals at the same time; one person directly responsible in the situation, the other person essentially detached from it. In such cases, it's usually desirable to choose the recommendation developed by the

person who will ultimately carry it out. He will then have a personal stake in proving that his idea is, in fact, workable. It's good administrative practice, therefore, to keep subordinates constantly aware of your willingness to have them work out their own solutions to problems in their particular operating areas.

18. *Build up subordinates' sense of the values of their work.* Most people need to think their jobs are important. Many even have to feel that they not only have an important job, but are essential in it, before they start clicking.

19. *Let your people know where they stand.* The day of "treat 'em rough and tell 'em nothing" has passed. A system providing periodic ratings for employees is the first step. However, the full value of such a system is realized only if ratings are discussed with each person individually so that each can bolster weak points, clear up misunderstandings, and recognize his particular talents.

A formal rating system may be worthwhile, but is not necessarily essential if the chief executive talks at least once a year with each assistant about his performance during the past period.

20. *Criticize or reprove in private.* This may, perhaps, seem obvious, but administrators forget to do it every day in hundreds of organizations. Reprimands in the presence of others cause humiliation and resentment instead of a desire to do better next time. Criticizing a subordinate when people from his department are present undermines his authority, his morale, and his enthusiasm to do his best for your company.

21. *Criticize or reprove constructively.* First, get all the facts; review them with those concerned, and reach an agreement on them. Then be ready to suggest a constructive course of action for the future. When you criticize, concentrate on the method or the results, not on personalities. If you can precede the criticism by a bit of honest praise, so much the better. Note, however, that some executives do this so regularly and unimaginatively that the compliments lose their value.

22. *Praise in public.* Most people thrive on appreciation. Praise before others often has a multiple impact. It tends to raise morale, increase prestige, and strengthen self-confidence—important factors in the development of capable junior officers. But be sure that those you praise are really the ones who deserve it, and that you don't encourage "credit grabbing."

23. *Pass the credit on down to the operating people.* Taking for yourself credit that really belongs to one of your operating people tends to destroy his initiative and willingness to take responsibility. Giving him fair recognition for what he does has a double benefit; he gets apprecia-

tion for doing a good job, and you get the help and support of a loyal staff. If you take all the bows when somebody else played the leading role, you can rapidly lose the respect of your executives.

24. *Accept moderate "griping" as healthy.* In small doses, griping can serve as a safety valve for your people. If they worked under a perfect administrator they would probably still complain, just because he *was* perfect. Vicious, personal sniping is, of course, another matter; here, you should make every effort to have the cause discovered and rooted out. Remember, too, that without some dissatisfaction there would be little incentive to do or get something better.

Communication, motivation, and supervision are all tied together. As owner/supervisor, you have to use each in order to effectively manage your employees. It isn't easy, and in the next chapter, on handling difficult situations, you'll see just how hard the job can be. When things go wrong, the emotional drain can be terrible. But when all runs smoothly, few things are more satisfying.

TWELVE

Handling Difficult Situations

*Absenteeism / Tardiness / Problem Employees / Decline
of Job Effectiveness / Criminal Behavior / Criticism /
Disciplining / Whether or Not to Keep an Employee /
Firing / Unionization and Grievances*

THERE COMES A TIME IN EVERY MANAGER'S LIFE WHEN managing people becomes intricate and difficult. Things don't go smoothly at all. Problems with your employees range from trivial to serious difficulties which can affect your business. These include:

- Absenteeism.
- Tardiness.
- Incompetence.
- Decline of effectiveness on the job.
- Criminal behavior.
- Criticizing employees.
- Disciplining employees.
- Deciding whether or not to retain a worker.
- Unionization and grievances.

You can run into one or more of these problems every day. Your job will be to correct the situation before it gets out of hand.

As a small business owner, you'll be working closely with all of your employees. Many will be your friends. You'll know about family crises, drinking problems, attitudes—in short, almost every factor that influences your employees' work. As a friend, you can commiserate and excuse, but as an employer you can't afford to be too lenient. You have to make business (not personal) decisions, because your business comes first. It must be protected and nourished. No one except you can do this.

Suppose a trusted employee, who is also a close friend, has been struggling with severe emotional problems. His wife has left him. He's made several bad investments, has gambled and is in hock up to his ears. For the past three weeks he has not even been marginally effective on the job. You have been carrying his load along with your own work. The situation can't go on—your business is suffering. What do you do?

It's a terrible problem. The man has worked for you for years. And it's not just a case of someone who can't do the job—he can do the job, and very well, too. But his private life is dragging him down.

You wear two hats. You're the man's boss. It isn't fair to your other employees, yourself, or your business to allow one person to contribute almost nothing. But you are also the man's friend, someone who understands and sympathizes.

It goes back and forth. Since you are his friend, how can you fire him during the worst time of his life? But you are the owner of a struggling business. How can you afford to carry deadwood for long?

You must think about the future. Is this a short-term problem, or will the situation go from terrible to unbearable?

There must be a cutoff line. You can bend over backwards to help out your friend, but not at the expense of your business. Unless the situation gets better, you'll have to let him go. It will be unpleasant and heart-wrenching, but it will have to be done.

That is what this chapter is all about—facing the unpleasant situations and working out the difficult problems you'll encounter as a small business owner/manager. Hopefully, with a well-managed business you won't be faced with these problems too often, but in one way or another some will appear—even in the best business.

ABSENTEEISM

Dave runs a newspaper delivery service. The routes have to be run from four to seven in the morning. Dave employees six drivers. For most, delivering papers is part-time work, a little extra money. In this business it is very hard to get people to stay more than a year or two.

Dave recognizes the problems of his labor market, but problems or no problems those papers must be delivered. There are no excuses for not delivering. Tim, one of Dave's employees, missed his route twice in one week. Dave had to cover the route himself. The first time Tim begged off, he telephoned Dave the night before. Dave was upset, but he accepted Tim's excuse— sick mother—and did the route. The second time Tim didn't even call. He just failed to show up. Dave tried to call him, but there was no answer. Later that day, Tim called Dave to apologize—his mother again. Dave warned Tim that he could not continue taking days off. He made it quite clear that Tim had had it. No more days off! All went well until the next week. Tim disappeared again, this time for three straight days.

After several futile phone calls, Dave sent Tim a note informing him that he was no longer employed by Dave's News Service. Two days later Tim showed up and pleaded with Dave to let him have his route back. Dave refused. By this time he had a new trainee who was learning Tim's old route. Tim was out.

Dave's business is not a conventional one in many ways. He must hire dependable employees, but he also has to put up with a high turnover because of the part-time nature of the job.

Tim's absenteeism was a serious problem—a business-threatening problem, if the absenteeism were allowed to continue unchecked. For Dave, the only solution was to fire Tim.

Absenteeism can be a serious problem in any business. It is especially deadly in a small business. One employee may be anywhere from 10 to 50 percent of the work force. His or her absence can throw the entire business out of kilter. A comparable situation would be the absence of 100 to 500 employees at a company which had 1,000 workers.

Absenteeism is difficult even with an excuse. Every manager dreads those nine o'clock calls where the employee (behind a barrage of coughs and sneezes) claims to be too sick to come to work. But absenteeism without an excuse is totally irresponsible. Even at the last minute, a boss can make arrangements to cover up for a missing employee—but if the boss never knows, what then? Is the employee late or absent? By the time the boss discovers the answer, a great deal of time has been wasted.

Keep track of every employee's absentee record. The record reveals two things: If a single employee has a high rate of absenteeism, then the fault probably lies with that employee, and your responsibility is to try to cure the employee. If a large percentage of your employees have severe absentee problems, then you should take a long look at your business to see what's wrong.

Sit down with the absentee offender and try to find out why. There are many reasons for absenteeism, ranging from job dissatisfaction to alcoholism. Remember, you have one goal—to stop this employee's absenteeism. If the problems are job-related, you can see if there are changes you can make. If the changes are impossible, then it's the employee you will have to change by getting another, more responsible one. If the problems are rooted in the employee's home life or personal behavior, the causes are out of your hands. As in the first case, you may sympathize with your employee, but there comes a time when enough is enough. Give the employee as much support as you can, but warn that the absenteeism can't continue. If the problem remains, your choice has been made for you. Fire away.

TARDINESS

Tardiness is first cousin to absenteeism. If the work is boring or unmotivating, tardiness will skyrocket. So tardiness is a good weathervane for detecting employee dissatisfaction.

Tardiness varies in seriousness from business to business. In some companies, fifteen to twenty minutes isn't noticed, but if an employee is late five minutes in others, a stiff reprimand will follow. If tardiness is a rare problem, you should overlook it. If it starts to become less rare, nip it in the bud. But be consistent. Follow the rules. You can't discipline one employee for being ten minutes late once and not do a thing about another employee who has been late a dozen times.

PROBLEM EMPLOYEES

Karen was hired to be an assembler in Seth's factory. She was marginal through her training period and didn't seem to be learning very quickly. But she seemed intelligent enough, so Seth decided to take a chance.

Karen was at the plant for three months. Her supervisor constantly complained that she was way behind in her work and wasn't doing even that little bit correctly. Much of her work had to be redone by someone else. The supervisor complained that this was leading to plenty of grumbling from the other workers who felt that Karen's work was holding them back.

Seth took a closer look. He had twelve employees and everyone had to pull their weight. Seth sat down and talked to Karen. He discovered that she was highly dissatisfied with her job. Being the youngest in her group, Karen had little in common with her co-workers. She also complained that her supervisor seemed to have it in for her—she was always breathing down her neck and picking her work apart.

Seth talked to the supervisor again. She denied Karen's accusations and restated that she thought Karen was just incapable of doing good work.

Seth then checked the production figures and watched Karen at work. She wasn't doing her job very well, but he still thought that she could if she were given the proper chance. Seth's factory had two groups, so he transferred Karen to the other one. The change worked. Karen adapted to the new situation well, and stayed with Seth.

Seth was lucky, in that his business was big enough to provide an alternative to letting Karen go. Large businesses can transfer a problem employee from one location to another—around the United States and overseas. Small businesses can't. When a small business owner has a problem employee, the choices are:

- Let things continue and suffer the consequences.
- Try to rehabilitate the problem employee—make him or her into a productive worker.
- Fire the employee.

DECLINE OF JOB EFFECTIVENESS

Decline of effectiveness is a serious problem in a small business. The opening section of this chapter showed just how serious. There aren't many options. A small business doesn't have the option of kicking the offender upstairs and out of the way. Your choices are the same three listed above.

You should give choice number two a serious effort before proceeding to number three. Decline in effectiveness can be related to many correctable problems, either at business or in the home. And correcting a problem makes more business sense than training someone new.

There is a difference if the decline of effectiveness is due to age or injury. For example, a fifty-five-year-old man with a heart condition can't be expected to continue working on the loading dock. Every attempt should be made to put him in another company position. If that is impossible, every effort must be made to place him in another company. Never desert an employee, especially one who has given your business a large part of his or her life. If you ruthlessly discard loyal employees, your reputation will plummet and relations with remaining employees will suffer.

CRIMINAL BEHAVIOR

You return to your office late one night to retrieve some forgotten papers. As you walk into the building, you bump into a clerk walking out with a box full of calculators and an electric typewriter. What do you do?

After taking back your property, you can fire him and call the police, or be lenient and just fire him. There is no room for a thief. This time it was office equipment. Next week, maybe a payroll, business secrets, or your wallet.

Criminal behavior can't be tolerated. This also goes for dope sellers and users, pilferers, saboteurs, etc. There is no rehabilitation for serious offenses committed against your business. Once the bond of trust has been broken, that's the end.

Of course, there is a difference between taking pencils and taking electric typewriters. You may find it advantageous to distribute pencils with the name of your business on them. But that's where you draw the line. Too much money is lost because of employee theft. So be strict with your property.

When you discover any serious behavior problem, start looking for a replacement. Fast. It isn't your job to continually police your employees. And do the next employer down the line a favor by refusing references. Suggest rehabilitation first.

The previous situations touch on a few of the multitude of employee offenses. Others are: horseplay on the job, talking too much, ignoring orders, leaving early, belligerency, creating general unpleasantness, poor attitude—the list can go on and on. How you react to these offenses is what is important. You should:

- Consider all facts.
- Listen carefully.
- Be consistent in rules and discipline.
- Be direct.
- Not get involved in a shouting match.

When an employee does something wrong—or doesn't do something right—you shouldn't rise up in righteous anger to smite the malefactor. Your job is to rectify the situation—to keep productivity high and the business rolling smoothly. There is no place for vendetta, revenge, or punishment because it feels good to you. When something goes wrong, try to act like a mechanic with a broken-down car. Analyze the situation and see where the disorder is, the reasons behind it, and the most efficient way to correct the disorder. That correction can take many forms—from revamping the entire business to casually criticizing a single employee.

You also have to be willing to face your own mistakes. Is the problem due to severe job dissatisfaction? Could you do a better job as manager? Don't immediately blame the employee. In the analysis of the problem, see if there is anything that points to you as the culprit. Maybe better communications, motivation, or supervision is in order—instead of a firing or demotion.

CRITICISM

There are ways to criticize your employees and ways not to.

Harriet, owner of a small public relations company, wanted a press release from her assistant, Ron, by eleven o'clock. She didn't get it. At 11:10 Harriet stormed out of her office and into the work area Ron shared with two secretaries and another assistant. Harriet, in an abusive manner, told Ron that he had five minutes to complete the release. She stormed back into her office and slammed the door. It sounded like a howitzer shot in the hushed office.

Five minutes later Ron dutifully handed Harriet the press release. When Ron started explaining, she curtly told him she was too busy to listen to his half-baked excuses. Ron left, outwardly calm but seething inside.

In addition to fueling Ron's righteous anger, Harriet sowed a feeling of insecurity into her other employees. Was she right or wrong?

Many owners would agree with Harriet. They feel it's good to build a fire under employees every once in a while. It is productive to criticize an employee, but it is never wise to humiliate one. Ron was humiliated. He was outraged that his boss would chew him out like that in front of co-workers. Harriet could have handled the situation just as well if she had called Ron into her office and discussed the problem. Ron obviously wasn't far behind the deadline, since he completed the job in five minutes.

Harriet had lost sight of her goals because of her own frustration and anger. And while she got her press release, she eventually lost Ron and her other assistant.

When you criticize someone:

- Do it in private.
- Allow the employee to present his or her side.
- Don't lose control of your temper or provoke the employee.

DISCIPLINING

A more serious problem is disciplining the employee. Discipline is punishment for some infraction of policy or rules. Some theorists believe that punishment does no good. They feel a heart-to-heart talk and a plan of action are far more valuable. However, the majority of businesses have rules and regulations—and penalties for not obeying those rules and regulations.

Before you go as far as punishing a worker, there are certain steps that have to be taken. First, you must find out all the facts in the case, just like a judge: What was the offense? who was involved? what are the excuses and stories? After you have found someone guilty, you must pick a punishment to fit the crime. Remember, you are trying to correct a situation. You are not being vindictive or revenging a wrong. Any punishment meted out has to be for the good of your business.

When you discipline an employee, be fair—and also be consistent. You can't dismiss one worker for a day and another for a week for the same offense. Keep a record of infractions. If one employee is continually being punished, investigate the underlying problem. If it can't be corrected, let the constant offender go.

Never forget, you are not engaged in a duel with any employee. You are trying to make a bad situation better.

WHETHER OR NOT TO KEEP AN EMPLOYEE

There comes a point when you must decide whether to keep or fire an employee. It's a simple matter of weighing all the facts:

- Has the employee worked for you long?
- Was the employee's work always poor, or is the poor performance recent?
- What is the employee's attitude?
- How much have you invested in the employee—would it be difficult to replace him or her?
- Does the employee hold a key position in your business?

Basically, what you are asking yourself is: "If I give this person more help, more time, or even another position, will he or she turn out to be an asset for the company?" And then you ask: "Is it worth it?"

If the employee is valuable, your answer may be yes. If the worker is new and has been bollixing up the job since the first day, your answer probably will be no.

Again, you are subjecting the questionable employee to a great deal of analysis—cool, dispassionate analysis. And you are also taking a close look at his or her job. Where don't the two fit? When the analysis has been completed, you should know whether or not you can upgrade the employee's work. If you can't, let the employee go.

FIRING

Dismissal of an employee is serious and shouldn't be done on a whim. But there are times when nothing else can be done.

You should look on firing as a necessary tool, something that will help your business. One of your workers can't cut it. Your only option is to let this person go. How do you cut the bonds?

Firing is messy emotionally. Many businesses psychologically pressure an unwanted employee out of the company. For example, an unwanted supervisor may be given the graveyard shift or assigned only tedious busy-work. The boss may snub the employee at every point, refusing even to talk to him. Pretty soon, the supervisor gets the point and quits. This tactic can be successful, but it takes time and has its own brand of unpleasantness. Also, some workers refuse to take the hint and fade out gracefully. They may be too dull to understand the subtleties, they may want to collect unemployment insurance, or they may not want to leave. Then you have to fire them, plain and simple.

Sandra ran a small department store in a midwestern town. Six salespersons worked for her in different departments. One employee, May, had been working at the store for two months. During that time she had been late fifteen times, taken six sick days, been absent twice, did not get along with three other employees, and had a terrible temper.

Sandra was a very quiet, mild-mannered individual who believed in giving her workers every conceivable chance. She talked to May privately several times and tried to get to the root of her problems. May explained that she came from a broken home and proceeded to give Sandra a real sob story. So Sandra covered for May when she didn't appear and tried to smooth out her relationships with the other salespeople.

Soon, Sandra's treatment of May began to irk the other employees. They saw May getting away with murder. They started grumbling, and their complaints worked their way back to Sandra. While she had sympathy for May's problems, she realized that if May didn't turn over a new leaf she would have to go.

The end came when Sandra caught May snapping at customers. She quietly told May to see her in her office at the end of the day. When May came in, Sandra immediately told her she was fired. She then proceeded to list the reasons for May's dismissal: tardiness, absenteeism, poor attitude, temper. Sandra spoke in an even tone at all times. She didn't sound angry, but she was firm. May cried and carried on for a few minutes. Sandra didn't budge. May changed her tactics, yelled at Sandra and threatened her. Sandra's expression didn't even change. The last thing Sandra wanted was a physical confrontation. So she remained impassive and told May that the interview was at a close and to go clean out her locker. May was beaten and she knew it. Her parting shot was that she was glad to get away from the crummy job.

Sandra had done a difficult thing well. She looked upon the task as something which had to be done and did it in a straight-forward, no-nonsense manner. What she had done was to:

- Make the decision to fire May.
- Collect all the facts, in case May challenged her.
- Have May report at the end of the day so she didn't disrupt work.
- Clearly state all the facts, leaving May no question as to whether she had been fired, and from what moment she could consider herself fired.
- Listen to all of May's arguments.
- Keep her temper, even when May became abusive.

You're human. With an employee like May you'd love to holler and get it out of your system. Don't. You could go too far with the wrong person. The worker who has just been fired has a lot of hostility bottled up, too. Never make a bad time worse by acting out your own rage.

Problems crop up whenever you work with people. It's part of the job. The trick is to stop the problem from growing into a bad situation. Hit it head on. Be firm, consistent, and decisive. After all, you're protecting your business.

UNIONIZATION AND GRIEVANCES

Unionization may or may not be classified as a serious problem. Usually, small businesses are immune—most organizers are after much bigger fish. But at times it does happen. And if your business does become unionized, it isn't the end of the world. Owners often feel unionization is a personal attack. It isn't necessarily—your employees may feel a very natural need to get more security.

The situation becomes difficult when grievances pop up. The union suddenly is there looking over your shoulder. The conflict is no longer between just you and the employee.

The best way to solve problems is face to face. Even if your business is unionized, this is a good procedure. The union becomes involved when the two parties can't resolve their difficulties alone. For example, you want to fire an employee because of his absenteeism. The employee feels you're being unfair and appeals to his union. You have to explain your side of the story to the union representative. If the representative feels the firing is warranted, end of story. If the case is disputed, you have to resolve the problem with the union. You can either fight it out and risk being struck, or you can compromise. At times, the union can force an unfair resolution, but if you approach the conflict with all the facts and don't act like a petulant adversary, you'll get your way—if you have been scrupulously fair.

As in the other cases, you must:

- Have all your facts at hand.
- Present them calmly.
- Be straightforward.

You have a union contract, so go by the rules. The union is there to protect the employees, not to make continual war upon management. If there is a fair solution, it should be reached.

THIRTEEN
Evaluating and Paying Employees

Paying the Employee / Job Evaluation

H OW ARE YOUR EMPLOYEES DOING ON THE JOB? DO YOU really know? A small business owner should always know how his or her workers are doing. Their progress is very important. It's difficult and time-consuming, but there are many rewards. Through constant evaluation, you can discover if your employees:

- Are satisfied or dissatisfied with their work.
- Should be recognized and rewarded for superior work.
- Can be motivated to increase general production.

Most employees welcome evaluation with open arms. If they're doing a good job, they want you to know about it. There are few things more frustrating than doing an excellent job without a hint of recognition. In fact, if you neglect to recognize and praise superior workmanship, you may just discover all of your employees working at roughly the same level. As the chapter on motivation indicated, everyone needs some form of recognition.

The performance review is also helpful to the worker falling behind. Constructive criticism is extremely useful. The worker may have a sense of uneasiness, but not know how to remedy his or her problem. A meeting with the boss may smooth things out—if the boss is on top of things. Offer criticism with an eye to straightening things out, not to chastise a wrongdoer.

A performance review also helps both the employee and the boss to set goals and standards for the future.

Evaluation shows the employee where he or she stands in the business. If an employee merits a promotion, a raise, or some other form of reward, you must recognize the effort. A small business can offer few special job titles—how many vice-presidents can a business with five employees have? So it's up to you to find ways of encouraging a good employee's behavior. Evaluation is the tool to use to discover who deserves what.

PAYING THE EMPLOYEE

A complex and baffling aspect of business is paying the people who work for you. The question is, how do you arrive at the magic number—in other words, how much is enough?

There are many factors involved:

- Will you pay wages or a salary?
- Does the worker earn a commission or tips?
- What are your competitors paying?
- How much does the government force you to pay?
- How much can you afford to pay?

Then you have to take a hard look at the job and the employee's performance:

- How much time and effort is involved?
- Is the work at all dangerous?
- How difficult is the job?
- How long has the employee worked for the business?

How much to pay employees is often perplexing. You have to satisfy your budget and your workers' pocketbooks. It gets worse if you have to satisfy a union as well. And employees can be very sensitive about how much everyone else makes, too. If one worker makes more than another, there better be an acceptable reason for the difference.

JOB EVALUATION

Job evaluation is the tool to use to make the first estimate about payments. The first step is to go back and look at your job analysis. Find out about all the basic job information. Check both the job description and job specifications, because you also need to know what skills the employee has and how valuable those skills are.

A job evaluation can be performed in a variety of ways, but most small businesses use the ranking system. This is simply comparing each job in your business and assigning it a rank. For example, you operate a small advertising agency. You have a head copywriter, two assistant copywriters, an artist, two secretaries, and a variety of part-time help. The head copywriter would rank highest, followed by the two assistants, the artist, the secretaries, and the part-time help.

After the job is ranked, the owner assigns the job a rate of pay. The higher the rank, the more pay.

This is only the beginning of the story, though. Other factors have to be considered:

- Do you pay by merit only, or do you take seniority into account?
- What type of benefits will you offer?
- How about paid vacation time?
- How many paid sick days?
- How much severance pay?
- Will you offer bonuses?
- What type of insurance packages will you offer?
- How about retirement funds?

It's a good idea to test the waters if you're uncertain about how much to pay. See what type of salaries or wages similar businesses pay. Also, look into their benefit plans.

Once you have worked out a payment plan, don't consider it unchangeable. And don't make it so rigid that it works against you. Some owners give a raise only after a certain time has elapsed, giving a terrific worker and an average worker the same increase after three months, six months, a year. After a year has passed, the terrific worker is earning the same as the chair-warmer. While money is not the biggest motivator, it can cause plenty of trouble. The diligent worker will quit or do less work. So build into your system a way to reward merit.

FOURTEEN

Working with Relatives

Fair Treatment for Nonfamily Employees / Unproductive Relatives / Management Checklist for a Family Business

THE BEST HAS BEEN SAVED FOR LAST. A HIGH PROPORTION of small businesses are family-owned. It's only natural. A father takes his son or daughter into the business, two brothers decide to pool their savings, a husband and wife decide to retire and open a small store, your Aunt Sophie demands that you make a place in your business for her son Manfred—the possibilities are mind-boggling. Small businesses are just often family affairs, as are many big businesses. Take a look at large corporations and see how many sons have been handed chairmanships by their powerful fathers.

Some family businesses have been run successfully. On the other hand, many have been shot down in flames *because* they were honeycombed with blood relatives. There are many reasons for failure—the elderly uncle who "loaned" the money to start the business suddenly wants it back, or worse, decides to tell his nephew how to run the business; one brother wants to diversify, the other wants to hold fast; a business flounders because the son who inherited it just isn't capable. These are all serious problems, but what this chapter is concerned with is the effects on people management. Of course, you can't completely separate all the functions of the small business, but there are special problems family-oriented businesses present to personnel management.

FAIR TREATMENT FOR NONFAMILY EMPLOYEES

The biggest problem is treating the nonfamily employees fairly. Ted operated a chain of three hardware stores with his cousin Sol. Sol's son Peter had just graduated from junior college and was hired to work in the family business.

At first, Ted was as pleased as Sol that Peter was coming into the business. Peter was immediately made an assistant manager at the main store. But Ted and Sol had nine other employees who had been working in the business for from two to six years. While they understood Peter's sudden rise to assistant manager, none of the passed-over employees were happy. Feelings like this pass, because it is almost universally recognized that while the boss' son may start at the bottom of the totem pole, he sure isn't going to take as much time to climb to the top. But Peter disturbed the other employees in other ways. He was seldom correct in his judgments and tried to throw his weight around. Worse, his father always backed him up or made excuses for him.

Two employees suddenly quit, and the picture became clearer to Ted, who had stayed out of the affair. He discovered that the employees had quit for one reason—Peter. Ted went to Sol to discuss the situation. He tried to be diplomatic, but Sol was furious. No matter what, his son Peter was going to continue as assistant manager and some day run the whole shooting match. Ted thought about Peter becoming his partner and stopped being diplomatic. He quickly arranged to sell his share of the business to Sol. Ted then invested in another business. Within a year, Peter left the store and went back to college to become a dentist, leaving Sol alone in the business.

Blood presents some very interesting and unusual problems. It's hard to be objective when your son or daughter is involved. And Sol's dream—like that of many fathers—was to have his son follow in his footsteps. Sol was willing to turn a blind eye to Peter's obvious incompetence. In doing so, he created a rift with his cousin Ted—a partnership which had worked successfully for eight years. And alienated his employees as well.

When a close relative is involved and a problem like Ted and Sol's pops up, a choice must be made. Which is more important—the continued smooth operation of the business, or your relative? A difficult question.

If you have nonfamily employees, you have to worry about them. What do you think would be the effect on morale if an employee was fired just to make room for a relative? If you want your business to be viable, you can't alienate nonrelatives. It isn't fair to them, and it certainly isn't fair to your business.

UNPRODUCTIVE RELATIVES

Another problem is working with the unproductive relative. What do you do with a nephew, cousin, brother, aunt, or grandmother who holds your business back? There's no kicking upstairs or transferring out of state in a small business. Nephew Harry is underfoot, day in, day out. A constant reminder of what a loser he is—and in your dollars and cents.

You're faced with a choice. Either you get rid of the relative and hire someone who can perform, or you continue to pour good money after bad. It's a question of priorities. If Harry collects a low salary and does busy work, you may be willing to put up with the minor headache. If your relatives are pressuring you to raise Harry's salary and make him vice-president, then dump him and forget about that side of the family.

Small family businesses can and do work. Cousin Gertrude just may turn out to be a whiz and worth every penny she gets. You usually can trust relatives with company assets. A relative will identify with your business and work harder to make it succeed.

There is no reason not to go into business with a relative as long as:

- You are compatible.
- You communicate easily.
- You agree about how the business will be run from the start.
- Duties are defined.
- You know who is boss.
- Everyone understands that the business comes first.

A family business can be a tremendous success. But it has to be run the same way any competitive business is run—for a profit.

Here's a Small Business Administration management checklist* for the family business:

MANAGEMENT CHECKLIST FOR A FAMILY BUSINESS

No small business is easy to manage, and this is especially true in a small family business. It is subject to all the problems that beset small companies, plus those that can, and often do, arise when relatives try to work together.

The family member who is charged with managing the company has to work at initiating and maintaining sound management practices. By describing what is to be done and under what circumstances, such practices help prevent some of the confusion and conflicts that may be perpetuated by self-centered family members. Such relatives sometimes regard the company as existing primarily to satisfy their desires.

The questions in this checklist are designed to help chief executive officers to review the management practices of their small family companies. The comments that follow each question are intended to stimulate thought rather than to include the many and various aspects suggested by the question.

	Yes	No
	☐	☐

Is executive time used on high priority tasks?
The time of the owner-manager is one of the most valuable assets of a small business. It should not be dribbled away in routine tasks that can be done as well, if not better, by other employees. Never lose sight of the fact that you, as owner-manager, have to make the judgments that will determine the success of your business. You may want to run a check on how your time is used. You can do so by keeping a log for the next several weeks. On a calendar memorandum pad, jot down what you do in half-hour or hour blocks. Then review your notes against the questions: Was my time spent on management tasks such as reviewing last week's sales figures and noting areas for improvement? Or did I let it dribble away on routine tasks such as opening the mail and sorting bills of lading? You may want to ask your key personnel to run the same sort of check on their time.

---

* U. S. Small Business Administration, Management Aid, No. 225, 1976.

	Yes	No

Do you set goals and objectives?
Goals and objectives help a small company to keep
headed toward profits. Goals and objectives should
be specific and realistic. In addition they should be
measurable, time-phased, and written. In getting a
list of your goals and objectives. start by writing
them out for your present successful operations.
Objectives that are written out in straightforward
language provide a basis for actions by your key personnel. For example, state that you will sell a certain
number of units this year rather than saying you will
increase sales.

	Yes	No

Do you have written policies?
Flag this question and return to it later. Working
through this checklist should suggest changes that
may be needed if you have written policies. By the
same token, your review of your business will provide input for writing out policies if there are none in
writing.

	Yes	No

***Is planning done to achieve these goals and objec-
tives?***
In a sense, planning is forecasting. An objective, for
example, for next year might be to increase your net
profit after taxes. To plan for it you need to forecast
sales volume, production of finished goods inventory, raw materials requirements, and all the other
elements connected with producing products and
selling them. Moreover, while planning your fore-
casts, you will want to make provision for watching
costs, including selling expenses. If there are key
employees who can provide input into the planning,
ask them to become involved in that process.

	Yes	No

***Do you test or check the reality of your goals and
plans with others?***
Outside advisers may spot "bugs" that you and your
people did not catch in the press of working through
the details of goal setting and planning.

	Yes	No

Are operations reviewed on a regular basis with the objective of reducing costs?

☐ Yes ☐ No

Costs must be kept in line for a profitable operation. Review operations periodically, such as weekly or monthly, to insure that overtime is not excessive, for example. And what about quality product acceptance by customers? Costs may be excessive because of obsolete methods or machinery that has seen its best days. And what about plant layout or materials flow? Can changes be made that will save time and materials? Determine the frequency of your reviews for the various types of operations, and place a tickler on your calendar to remind you of these review dates.

Are products reviewed regularly with the objective of improving them?

☐ Yes ☐ No

Products as your customers benefit from them are the key to repeat sales. A regular review of your products helps to keep them up to the expectation of customers. Feedback from customers can be useful here. To reduce costs, sometimes a product can be modified without sacrificing use and quality. If product obsolescence is a hazard, what plans are being made to substitute new products as existing ones become obsolete?

Do you ask outside advisers for their opinions and suggestions on products and operation procedures?

☐ Yes ☐ No

Outside persons, such as friends in noncompeting lines of business and management personnel from local colleges and universities, can help you see the facts about your products and operating procedures. They can provide a fresh viewpoint—the viewpoint of persons who are not involved in the products and operations as are you and your key personnel. The suggestions and counsel from a local management consultant may provide benefits far in excess of his or her cost. In this area, some small companies set up a board of directors to satisfy the law concerning small corporations. But that is the end of it. Members of the board are not used for their knowledge and skill in business. They can make valuable contributions, and the owner-manager should use all possible opportunities for getting such concerned opinions about the various phases of the company.

	Yes	No

Are marketing and distribution policies and procedures reviewed periodically? ☐ ☐

The best-made product in the world can run into trouble if marketing and distribution policies and procedures are not right for it. Periodic checks can help you to be aware of changes that may be taking place in the channels through which you distribute. One approach is to check your competition; does it seem to be changing channels and policies? Can you still meet the requirements of your customers by using your traditional channels of distribution?

	Yes	No

Are there periodic reviews of profit-and-loss statements and other financial reports? ☐ ☐

In these reviews you can compare your operating ratios to those for your industry. It is also helpful to review your cash flow projections to see what, if any, changes are needed in your financial planning.

	Yes	No

Do you need an organization chart? ☐ ☐

You may need only a simple organization chart to show accountability and to establish a chain of command. In a family business, accountability and chain of command should be spelled out so that the one who is the chief executive of the company has the "mandate" he or she needs for managing.

	Yes	No

Do you use job descriptions for your key personnel? ☐ ☐

When you and your key personnel write descriptions for their jobs, you and they have a clear understanding of what is to be done and by whom. Such an understanding is essential in any small business, but especially critical when relatives are involved. Spelling out duties may not prevent conflicts with you and an in-law, but such detail can help you resolve misunderstandings, if and when they occur. In addition, when, and if, a key person leaves, the job description is a helpful tool in recruiting and training a replacement.

	Yes	No
	☐	☐

Do you periodically compare performance of key personnel with their job descriptions?
Periodic comparison of performance helps your key personnel to be efficient. It also helps to pinpoint weak spots for you and them to work on for improvement.

	Yes	No
	☐	☐

Do you provide opportunities for key personnel to grow?
Your aim should be to help key personnel stay alert to new and more efficient ways to do things. Conferences, seminars, and workshops which trade associations and agencies, such as the Small Business Administration, sponsor can help key personnel to grow in their management skills and outlook. Rotating job assignments is a way to make key personnel aware of the problems that their counterparts face. Include in your budget an amount that can be spent during the year for personnel training and education.

	Yes	No
	☐	☐

Do you face the issue when key personnel stop growing?
Some owner-managers try to avoid the unpleasant task of facing the fact that a key person has stopped growing. It may be the result of not matching personnel and the job. Or in some family businesses, the cousin or brother-in-law never was interested in personal growth or any aspects of management. If there is little or nothing you can do about such a mismatch, face it and don't waste time trying to do the impossible. On the other hand, outside problems may be crowding in on the key person. Once you know why he or she stopped growing, you can deter-

mine what needs to be done. In some cases, additional training is the answer. In other cases, the motivation that results from broadened job responsibilities resolves the problem.

	Yes	No

Are there policies and plans for motivating employees?

☐ Yes ☐ No

Working through others is by no means an easy task. First of all, people are not puppets that can be moved by strings. Life may be a stage, as the poet said, but most people in small business are reluctant to submit to directors. Look for ways—good communications, respect for their viewpoint, incentive pay, and so on—to encourage people to *want* to do what you *need* them to do as employees in your company.

Do you have adequate employee benefit plans?

☐ Yes ☐ No

This includes life and health insurance, major medical, and pension. Benefit plans often are necessary to meet competition for skilled employees. Substantial plans can help to hold nonfamily key individuals in a family-owned business.

Do you have key personnel insurance on yourself, and is your family protected against your untimely passing?

☐ Yes ☐ No

If these precautions are not taken, your death could result in the rapid dissolution of the business.

Is there lack of communication among key personnel?

☐ Yes ☐ No

The routine passing of information among you and your key personnel may be all that you want it to be. But what about disagreement? Do key personnel refrain from expressing disagreement with you? Good communications should provide a forum for exchanging ideas and for airing differences of opinion. Possibly an early-morning meeting once a week with you and your key personnel would provide a forum for exchanging ideas.

	Yes	No

Does your record-keeping system present a realistic picture of your business? Is this the same type of record-keeping system that other companies in your industry commonly use?

| | ☐ | ☐ |

Appropriate records should give the owner-manager answers to questions such as: Is there sufficient cash to operate the business? To pay back the bank? To pay taxes? Is too much capital tied up in inventory? Are accounts receivable being collected promptly? Bankers and other lenders need a realistic picture. Corporate records, if your company is a corporation, should be up-to-date, including corporate minutes and record books. In checking out your record-keeping, keep in mind that a poor system can result in excessive and meaningless information.

	Yes	No

Do you seek legal and financial advice on major transactions?

| | ☐ | ☐ |

The fine print in contracts causes trouble for some small business owners. They did not realize until it was too late what they had agreed to do. Legal and financial advice at the appropriate time can help the owner-manager to comprehend the full scope of his company's contractual obligations and allow him to make decisions based on facts rather than assumptions. Whenever possible, use your standardized contract in making contractual obligations.

	Yes	No

Do you document informal agreements with customers, suppliers, and others?

| | ☐ | ☐ |

"He's as good as his word" is a fine attitude to have about customers, suppliers and others with whom you work on a daily basis. But think a moment; in being "as good as your word," how often do you forget? Memory slips. A note to yourself, or to a supplier, to confirm a telephone conversation, for example, helps both of you to recall what you agreed, or did not agree, upon, and prevents misunderstanding and hard feeling. Keep dated copies of all correspondence you send out. At some later period these copies could be invaluable.

	Yes	No

Do you plan your major financial decisions with the help of your accountant, lawyer, and other tax advisers?

An owner-manager cannot ignore the impact of federal and state income taxes, as well as other taxes, on his business. He should plan his major financial decisions with the help of his accountant, lawyer, and other tax advisers.

	Yes	No

Do your plans include self-development projects for yourself?

Sometimes an owner-manager sets up training for everyone in his company except himself. Because conditions change so rapidly, he should set aside some time for activities that will help him to keep abreast of his industry and the economic world in which his company operates. Your trade association should be a source about meetings, conferences, and seminars which you can use in such a program for yourself.

	Yes	No

Are there plans for succession in the event of the untimely death of the family member who manages the company?

The successor may not be the same person who substitutes when the chief executive officer is sick or on vacation. Whether the successor is a family member or a nonfamily employee, the business should make the transition smoother when the family agrees upon a successor ahead of time. Such agreement is necessary if the business is to bear the expense of grooming the successor.

lusion

MANAGING PEOPLE IS MADDENING, FRUSTRATING, TIRING, and, if you do it right, very rewarding. Since you own a small business, you'll be in the midst of your employees all the time. Managing then can be pleasant for you and them, or a full-time war with plenty of casualties. If you are careful in selecting, training, and managing, your business will prosper. If you don't pay any attention to the people working for you, you probably won't have a business very long. You are the one who can make the difference. You must make an all-out effort.

The contents of this book are interrelated. You can't hire someone and then forget about him or her. You can't take bodies off the street, subject them to intensive training, and expect top-notch employees. And you can't ignore your employees once they are trained and on the job. You have to become a full-time people manager on top of your other duties.

This book has indicated a path through some of the intricacies of people management. It's up to you to follow that path.

Suggested Reading

Beach, Dale S., *Personnel: The Management of People at Work* (New York: Macmillan, 1974).

Broom, Halsy N., *Small Business Management* (Cincinnati: Southwestern, 1971).

Chruden, Herbert J., and Arthur W. Sherman, *Personnel Management* (Cincinnati: Southwestern, 1976).

Cone, William F., *Supervising Employees Effectively* (Reading, Mass.: Addison-Wesley, 1974).

Cooper, Alfred M., *How to Supervise People* (New York: McGraw-Hill, 1973).

Crane, Donald, *Personnel Management: A Situational Approach* (Belmont, Calif.: Wadsworth, 1974).

Davies, Ivor K., *The Organization of Training* (New York: McGraw-Hill, 1973).

Doyle, Dennis M., *Efficient Accounting and Record-Keeping* (New York: Wiley, 1977).

Jucius, Michael J., *Personnel Management* (Homewood, Ill.: Irwin, 1975).

Loffel, Egon W., *Protecting Your Business* (New York: Wiley, 1977).

Petrof, John, *Small Business Management* (New York: McGraw-Hill, 1972).

Pickle, Hal B., *Small Business Management* (New York: Wiley, 1976).

Richards, Gerald F., *Tax Planning Opportunities* (New York: Wiley, 1977).

Richman, Eugene, *Practical Guide To Managing People* (Englewood Cliffs, N.J.: Prentice-Hall, 1975).

Seder, John W., *Credit and Collections* (New York: Wiley, 1977).

Steinhoff, Dan, *Small Business Management Fundamentals* (New York: McGraw-Hill, 1974).

Sweet, Don, *The Modern Employment Function* (Reading, Mass.: Addison-Wesley, 1973).

Wayne, William, *How to Succeed in Business When the Chips Are Down* (New York: McGraw-Hill, 1972).

Weiss, W. H., *The Art and Skill of Managing People* (Englewood Cliffs, N.J.: Prentice-Hall, 1975).

INDEX